THE

FAKE CHINA THREAT

AND ITS VERY REAL
DANGER

by JOSEPH SOLIS-MULLEN

The
LIBERTARIAN
INSTITUTE

THE

FAKE
CHINA
THREAT

AND ITS VERY REAL
DANGER

The Fake China Threat and Its Very Real Danger

Cover Design © 2023 by Andrew Zehnder

Published in the United States of America by

The Libertarian Institute
612 W. 34th St.
Austin, TX 78705

LibertarianInstitute.org

ISBN 13: 979-8-9884031-3-5

"It is the responsibility of intellectuals
to speak truth and expose lies."

– Noam Chomsky, 1967
"The Responsibility of Intellectuals"

For future generations:
that they might be.

Praise for *The Fake China Threat*

"Joseph Solis-Mullen has done America a great favor by writing this great book about the hype surrounding the allegedly dangerous rise of Chinese power in the Pacific [...] this threat is not all it's cracked up to be."
— Scott Horton, Director of the Libertarian Institute

"Joseph Solis-Mullen vividly captures the folly of politicians, pundits, and policymakers who are pushing the United States towards an unnecessary military confrontation with China. Exaggerating the Chinese threat is already spurring idiotic U.S. corporate subsidies and far worse could follow."
— Jim Bovard, USA Today columnist and Fellow at the Libertarian Institute

"In less than 100 pages, Solis-Mullen dismantles the misconceptions surrounding China, offering vital facts and context often overlooked by Americans [...] This book is a must-read for those seeking a better understanding of what may be the most consequential issue of our time."
— Dave DeCamp, host of Antiwar News

"Joseph Solis-Mullen does more to undermine the claim that there is this threat in his short but elegant and eloquent book, The Fake China Threat and Its Very Real Danger, than other much longer tomes. It is thorough, it is well written, it is a pleasure to read."
— Dr. Walter E. Block, Professor of Economics at Loyola University

"In his succinct, well-written, and thoroughly convincing book, Solis-Mullen incisively debunks the China threat by exploring China's history, the history of American intervention in Chinese affairs, and China's substantial, but underdiscussed, internal problems and external constraints."
— Dr. Ivan Eland, Senior Fellow at the Independent Institute

"China, like most of Asia, is a mystery to most Americans. This book solves the mystery and throws the truth into sharp relief. The last thing Chinese leaders want is a war with any foreign power. Everyone who can should read this book."
— Douglas Macgregor, Col (ret) U.S.A, author of *Margin of Victory*

"Give this book to the next person in your life who mouths off about the fake China Threat [...] Solis-Mullen's authoritative and extremely well-sourced book is a necessary primer for any objective and sound understanding of U.S.-China Relations."
— Matthew Hoh, Associate Director of the Eisenhower Media Network

Table of Contents

Map and Key Facts

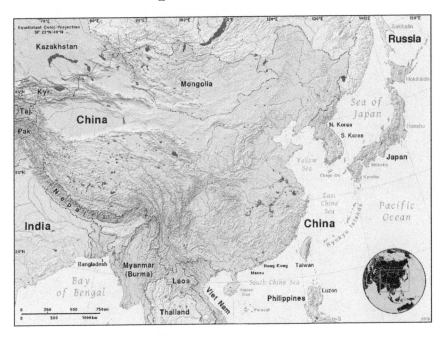

Distance from Taiwan to the Mainland…	81 miles / 130 kilometers
Distance from Guam to Taiwan…	1,711 miles / 2,754 kilometers
Distance from Hawaii to Taiwan…	5,276 miles / 8,491 kilometers
Minimum Cruise Missile Range…	621 miles / 1,000 kilometers
Maximum Cruise Missile Range…	1,864+ miles / 3,000+ kilometers
China's Land-Based Missile Forces…	9 major systems / 425 launchers
Number of Chinese "Carrier Killers"…	30
Avg. Number of Personnel on a *Nimitz*-Class Carrier…	6,000
Total Number of Active U.S. Carriers (All Types)…	20

Preface and Acknowledgments

Critics of the increasingly bipartisan consensus surrounding conflict with China face a difficult task. For the fake China Threat is not a single concrete thing that can be pointed to or otherwise signified. Rather, as a manufactured thought climate produced by a series of interlocking incentive structures, like Kafka's Castle it looms inscrutable, but no less ominous for that. Upon close inspection, however, the inner workings of the fake China Threat reveal nothing new about the anatomy of the state and its concordant logic.

On the one hand, it serves as a legitimating device, a new reason for the continually climbing defense budgets, new toys for generals and admirals, and overseas bases; for the continued meddling by comfortably ensconced State Department officials in the affairs of other states; and the existence of an intrusive national security apparatus. Stoking a climate of uncertainty and fear, representatives of the state spin conflicts thousands of miles away as looming threats to everyday Americans in order to justify their continued position of power over them, with a well-funded network of think tanks and corporate press helping to prescribe the acceptable limits of public discourse in order to marginalize dissent.

On the other hand, the fake China Threat serves as a convenient scapegoat for the end results of the bad policies Washington has itself authored and for decades pursued. America deindustrialized? China's fault. Millions of Americans hooked on drugs? China's fault. The Saudis and Iranians don't want the Americans around anymore? China's fault. Et cetera.

There is one element of truth to the fake China Threat, however: the existence of an independent China (or Russia) is a threat to Washington's accustomed ability to do more or less whatever it wants, wherever it wants. But the existence of an independent China is already a fact. Refusal on the part of Washington to accept it will cause more than theoretical problems, and therein lies the real danger.

As Washington increasingly pivots away from understandings brokered and signed off on decades ago by the leading representatives of both parties, beginning with Richard Nixon and concluding with Jimmy Carter, the slow erosion of the so-called "One China" policy and "strategic ambiguity" is being met with hostility by a Beijing now fully capable of getting what it wants in its immediate neighborhood.[1] Its simulated blockade of Taiwan in the late summer of 2022 following the ill-advised visit by then-Speaker of the House Nancy Pelosi (D–CA) was a taste of things to come in the South China Sea. With claims of "inevitable" war between the U.S. and China becoming the regular fodder of newspaper editorials and morning talk shows, the purpose of this short book is to put in one place and in concise form the arguments for why the American people are not served by confrontation with China. The task is an urgent one, for while states like India or Japan may have their own reasons for wanting the United States around as a balancer against an increasingly robust neighbor, those reasons are not in line with the interests of the American people and never will be.

When Noam Chomsky wrote that intellectuals living in free societies were in a position to expose the lies of governments, he was careful to distinguish between statist intellectuals like Martin Heidegger or Arthur Schlesinger, Jr., and those who "seek the truth lying hidden behind the veil of distortion and misrepresentation, ideology and class interest, through which the events of current history are presented to us." This, then, is the present task.

Writing a book is never a solo effort, and with five young children I could not have done this without the patient support of my wife, Alexandria.

Special thanks are due to Keith Knight, Scott Horton, Kyle Anzalone, Connor Freeman, Dave DeCamp, Patrick Macfarlane, Ryan McMaken, William Anderson, and Kyle Matovich.

Many thanks to my copyeditor Ben Parker, and also to Mike Dworski and Grant F. Smith, for readying this book for publication. I would also like to thank Andrew Zehnder for designing the cover art.

---

[1] James Lee, "The One-China Policy in Transition," *Georgetown Journal of International Affairs*, November 9, 2022.

Author's Note

It was necessary in the course of writing this book to address concerns the author personally finds irrelevant or entirely specious. For, to paraphrase Lincoln, all the armies of the world could not with all their effort take a single drink from the Ohio or Potomac, so secure is the continental United States in its borders. The fact is, however, that as libertarian realists[2] my colleagues and I are in the overwhelming minority, and attempts to shift the Overton Window regarding the fake China Threat without making certain of the cases contained herein (for example, regarding China's internal weaknesses and external challenges) will invariably result in a less convincing argument against the increasingly bipartisan consensus in Washington, D.C., of the necessity or inevitability of conflict with China.

It is, in short, necessary but not sufficient simply to state axiomatically that what happens in China or Southeast Asia is none of Washington's business, or that the overly militarized foreign policy of the United States is largely driven by domestic political concerns. So built up in the imagination of many Americans has been the threat China allegedly poses to them and their families, that the determined opponent of the fake China Threat must venture onto the tiresome grounds of so-called "Great Power competition." He must then make estimations of relative power that, as it happens, largely buttress the case against Washington doing anything other than seeking normal relations with Beijing. Not being a Sinologist, a member of the foreign policy establishment, or in the pay of any who benefit from war or the preparation for it, I have no conflicts of interest to state. As a political scientist, economist, historian, and American, it is the lives, liberty, property, and prosperity of my fellow Americans that I seek to defend in doing what I can to discredit the fake China Threat. Aware that long-form reading is dying out, every effort has been made to keep this tract as short as possible.

---

[2] Justin Raimondo "Looking at the 'Big Picture,' Libertarian Realism: A Theory of Foreign Relations," Antiwar.com, November 10, 2011.

Introduction

From the front pages of the *Washington Post* and *Wall Street Journal, Foreign Affairs*, the *Economist*, to the *New York Times*'s Best Sellers List; from CNN and MSNBC to FOX and NEWSMAX; from think tanks to Pentagon planners, Congressional testimonies and White House statements: *CHINA!* So singularly focused and omnipresent has the narrative of the fake China Threat become, that one can be forgiven for forgetting that China is in fact a middle-income country of modest capabilities and with no stated intention of doing any harm to Americans or the United States; further, that China is not bent on world domination; and further still, as shall be clearly demonstrated, even if it were surreptitiously desirous of obtaining such global hegemony, there is a negligible chance of that coming to pass, whatever Beijing's efforts. The reasons for this are many. From China's own internal problems, including a lack of critical resources, a dependence on external markets, a lopsided demography, combative ethnic minorities, resentful elites, an ongoing economic slowdown, and a possible economic collapse — to China's daunting external problems, from its lengthy borders and limited access to the Indian and Pacific Oceans, to the number of neighboring states that are either uneasy about an increasingly powerful China or seeking to counter outright or otherwise to impede its rise. These include India, Japan, Australia, South Korea, the Philippines, Vietnam, and Indonesia. This is to say nothing of Taiwan, officially recognized by both the UN and Washington as a breakaway region of China, and which stands as the most serious point of transitional friction at present.

While China is growing more relatively powerful, much of the very real danger that exists in the region stems from attempts by its aforementioned neighbors to balance against a more assertive Beijing — which, as it has grown more relatively powerful, has begun to press its own interests more forcefully in dealing with its neighbors, as well as with more distant powers such as the United States. This last is particularly important. For while planners in Beijing believe that the gravitational pull of its enormous and still growing economy will eventually allow it to get what it wants from its neighbors, the United States stands alone as the one country that cannot be bought off or bullied in this way. Further, as will be detailed, much of China's newfound assertiveness stems directly from the increased sense of threat it feels vis-à-vis the United States. It is in its attempts to push back against the United States that Beijing has ultimately alarmed many of its neighbors. Why Beijing has reacted so strongly to Washington's continued activities in the region requires an appreciation of the history between the two states. Therefore, before detailing the myriad reasons why China won't be taking over the world or even likely enjoying the kind of undisputed regional hegemony the United States has enjoyed for over a century, and why Washington should be pursuing a policy of restraint in dealing with China, it is first necessary to appreciate the extent to which the United States has been involved in meddling in domestic Chinese affairs. This will allow readers to understand how Washington's broader policies toward China have negatively shaped Chinese perceptions of the United States and its intentions toward China, and how it is these actions that have created what few real dangers exist.

Chapter 1:
A Brief History of Sino–U.S. Relations

Western interventions in domestic Chinese affairs began in earnest in 1842, when the British Empire forced open the country following the end of the First Opium War.[3] Access to trade, immunity for its nationals from Chinese law, and entry of Christian missionaries were forced on a faltering Qing dynasty — to say nothing of the tons of opium that flooded into China. Although successive U.S. administrations officially protested, they insisted on the same privileges for itself and its merchants as those enjoyed by the European empires. This was the so-called "Open Door" policy, eventually articulated by Secretary of State John Hay. Bostonian merchants in particular made good trade running Ottoman opium to China. The Second Opium War, which broke out in 1856, actually featured American forces fighting alongside the British at the Battles of the Barrier Forts (1856) and Taku Forts (1860). Such U.S. military assistance to the European empires in their depredations of China would continue, with Washington helping to put down the Boxer Rebellion at the turn of the century, occupying Peking (Beijing) and extracting a large indemnity for itself.[4]

With the fall of the Qing dynasty and the birth of the Republic of China (1912), there was hope on both the Chinese right and left that U.S. policy toward China might change. But despite having initially signaled support for the restoration of at least the German-occupied parts of China to the young Republican government in exchange for their dispatch of perhaps as many as 100,000 Chinese laborers to assist the Allied war effort on the Western Front, at Versailles U.S. President Woodrow Wilson abandoned the idealism of his vaunted Fourteen Points, instead granting the former

---

[3] Interested readers can see Mao Haijian's *The Qing Empire and the Opium War: The Collapse of the Heavenly Dynasty* (2018), Peter Ward Fay's *The Opium War (1840–1842): Barbarians in the Celestial Empire in the Early Part of the Nineteenth Century and the War by Which They Forced Her Gates Ajar* (originally published in 1975, republished in 1998); or they can consult Arthur Waley's even earlier *The Opium War through Chinese Eyes* (originally published in 1958, republished in 2005).

[4] Those specifically interested in the United States' role in "opening up" China can actually find a frankly unabashed chronicle on the State Department's own Office of the Historian webpage (see Works Cited).

German Imperial holdings to the Japanese.[5] A nominal wartime ally, the rapidly expanding Japanese Empire had opportunistically occupied German possessions in Asia once hostilities in Europe commenced, and Wilson used the recognition of Tokyo's claims as leverage to buy Japanese involvement in his League of Nations project. As for fledgling Republican China's other petitions — that the unequal treaties imposed following the Opium Wars be abolished and control of its revenue collection returned to Chinese authorities — these too were denied. This led a young Mao Zedong, formerly a rabid Wilsonian, to call the Americans "a bunch of robbers who only cynically champion self-determination."[6]

The disillusion with America and its purported idealism continued into the 1920s, with Warren Harding's administration declining to recognize the uneasy coalition of Republican and Communist forces under the loose leadership of Sun Yat-sen, opting instead to recognize a series of feuding warlords who happened to seize control of the capital, Peking.[7] It was only with the defeat of the warlords and the subsequent split between the Chinese right and left, precipitated by the former under the new leadership of Chiang Kai-shek, that the familiar Cold War and present-day alignments began to take shape — with Moscow and the Chinese Communist Party (CCP) on one side and Washington and the Republic of China (ROC) on the other. The latter partnership was particularly slow in developing, however, with the American public distracted by the Great Depression and disillusioned by the apparently pointless deaths of over 100,000 Americans in World War I. Content to let the warring Chinese and Japanese bleed one another throughout the 1930s and early 1940s, it wasn't until near the conclusion of the U.S. Pacific theater campaign against the Japanese that

---

[5] Paul French provides an excellent, if at times reductive, book-length treatment to the topic in his *Betrayal in Paris: How the Treaty of Versailles Led to China's Long Revolution* (2016). Although it is worth noting that at the very same time the various Western governments reneged on their promises, Lenin renounced all of Soviet Russia's extraterritorial rights in China, leading directly to the May Fourth Movement and the increased credibility of communism in China.

[6] This quotation comes from former Australian Prime Minister, and Sinologist, Kevin Rudd's comparatively worthy *The Avoidable War? The Dangers of a Catastrophic Conflict between the U.S. and China* (2022).

[7] This again contrasted sharply with the Soviets, who provided money, arms, and training to the struggling alliance of the Chinese left and right — the Kuomintang and CCP — at least until the former, under the new leadership of Chang Kai-shek, turned on the CCP in 1927.

real aid started to flow to the corrupt, ineffectual, and dictatorial Chiang Kai-shek and his nominally Republican forces. Though the aid would continue in the years immediately following the Japanese surrender, it was clear, particularly to George Marshall, who visited China to encourage a reconciliation between the Kuomintang (KMT) and the CCP, that good money was being thrown after bad.[8]

With the triumph of the CCP in 1949, the so-called "loss of China," and the retreat of Chiang Kai-shek and his followers to the fortress island of Formosa (Taiwan), successive U.S. administrations beginning with that of Harry Truman effectively prevented the conclusion of the decades-long Chinese Civil War by using American naval power to defend the Taiwan Straits, and further refused to recognize the Communist government now in place in Beijing. These policies continued with little change over the following two decades, and included hot conflict between the two in Korea (1950–53), as well as proxy conflict in Vietnam (1955–75). That is, until President Richard Nixon and National Security Advisor Henry Kissinger recognized that the apparently monolithic communist front in Eurasia was in fact split along sharply nationalist lines, with the Chinese refusing to follow Moscow's directives by the late 1950s at the absolute latest and openly competing for influence in the Third World by the mid-1960s.[9] Nixon's secret trip to Beijing and the Three Communiques that followed (in 1972, 1979, and 1982) formed the basis for the eventual normalization of relations and the recognition of the Chinese Communist Party's legitimacy by Jimmy Carter in 1978, as well as sought to define the contours of their relationship going forward.[10] The communiques, focused exclusively on U.S. respect for China's sovereignty, required the U.S. to

---

[8] See British historian Michael Lynch's *The Chinese Civil War (1945–49)* or, for a more comprehensive depiction of what was in effect a decades-long struggle, the Dutch historian Hans van de Ven's *China at War: Triumph and Tragedy in the Emergence of the New China*; while Cold War historian Odd Arne Westad's *Decisive Encounters: The Chinese Civil War (1946–50)* pays special note to the impact and interplay of Sino-American relations.

[9] For a contemporaneous account, see Donald Zagoria's *The Sino-Soviet Conflict (1956–61): The Widening Breach Between the Russian and Chinese Communists* (1964); while those interested in Kissinger's own account can consult the more recent *On China* (2011).

[10] The texts of each of the three joint statements is available in a single document, put together by Brown University's Watson Institute for International Studies (see Works Cited).

break off diplomatic relations with Taiwan, eliminate its military treaty with Taipei, and agree not to station U.S. forces on the island — now officially recognized by Washington, as well as the UN, as part of China. While Beijing never renounced the potential for the use of force in the event that Taiwan ever declared independence, they were now committed with Washington to try to work with Taipei to bring about peaceful reunification.

Nixon's opening to China had been premised on the idea of using Beijing to balance against the Soviet Union, a strategy followed by each of his predecessors all the way to the end of the first Cold War approximately a decade and a half later. With the death of Mao and the ensuing struggle for power having been won by the reformer Deng Xiaoping, China gradually opened up to foreign trade and investment and began to experiment with markets, prices, and private ownership of the means of production. So began the most incredible period of economic development the world has ever witnessed, with a billion Chinese eventually raised from the lowest levels of poverty to the position of an industrialized and rising middle-income society by the late 2000s.

In the meantime, however, with the end of the first Cold War and the disintegration of the Soviet Union a few years later, the logic of Nixon and Kissinger's strategy of using China to balance the Soviet Union no longer held. U.S. policymakers had a new idea, however: integrating China into the U.S.-created and U.S.-dominated global institutional order would make China a "responsible stakeholder," and with time, as the country grew wealthier and more integrated, this would lead to its liberalization and democratization. But this did not happen. Instead, it granted the Communists in Beijing legitimacy at home as a provider of material well-being; while, as China's economic power increased, so, too, did its military capabilities, and rather than focusing on aircraft carriers and other power projection capabilities, People's Liberation Army (PLA) planners instead focused on building up an area denial capability sufficient to deter any potential U.S. intervention in the event of a war between Beijing and Taipei, whose independence the CCP leadership view as the final remnant of China's "century of humiliations," the last impediment to the full restoration of Chinese sovereignty.

Chapter 2:
The View from Beijing

Though open hostility between the two officially ceased with the normalization of relations between Washington and Beijing — indeed they even partnered to punish the Vietnamese for intervening to remove the murderous Khmer Rouge regime in Cambodia (1979) — relations between the two were quickly complicated by continued U.S. interference in Chinese domestic affairs: from Congressional sanctions over Tiananmen (1989), to U.S. actions during the Third Taiwan Straits Crisis (1996), to the gradual erosion by Washington of the spirit if not the letter of the Three Communiques,[11] to sanctions on Beijing for its treatment of ethnic minorities such as the Tibetans and Uyghurs. The sense in Beijing of a China under threat was reflected in its reorientation of military planning in the 1990s and early 2000s, when its attention shifted away from preparing to fight massive land campaigns against its Eurasian neighbors to focusing first and foremost on a future conflict with the United States in Southeast Asia.[12] Again, this was particularly so with respect to Taiwan, which the U.S. never officially ruled out militarily intervening to defend under the tactic of "strategic ambiguity."[13] U.S. interventions in the post-Cold War era, from Iraq to Serbia, increased this sense of urgency for CCP planners. In the case of the First Iraq War, or "Operation Desert Storm," Washington's demonstration of the so-called "revolution in military affairs" highlighted the gap between the two in military capabilities; while in Serbia,

---

[11] For example, U.S. officials and representatives hosting or attending high-level diplomatic meetings with Taiwanese leaders, constructing an embassy in all but name in Taipei, and placing U.S. troops on the island.

[12] M.G. Yevtodyeva, "Development of the Chinese A2/AD System in the Context of U.S.-China Relations," published in 2022 in the *Herald of the Russian Academy of Sciences*; David Shambough, "China's Military in Transition: Politics, Professionalism, Procurement, and Power Projection," published in 1996 in *The China Quarterly*; or the Rand Corporation's 2015 study "China's Incomplete Military Transformation."

[13] Worth noting, since taking office in 2020 Biden has repeatedly made statements apparently clarifying U.S. intention to intervene in the event of an invasion or blockade by Beijing, a departure from the prior policy aimed at keeping both Taipei and Beijing guessing as to Washington's intentions and thereby attempting to stay both.

Washington's willingness to ignore the UN and act unilaterally was compounded by its allegedly accidental attack on the Chinese embassy in Belgrade, which killed multiple Chinese nationals.

But just as Beijing was ramping up its own capabilities on the back of an ascendent economy resultant from its integration into the global capitalist system, Washington's apparent "hyperpower" was dealt a series of serious self-inflicted blows. Beginning with the Second Iraq War and the invasion of Afghanistan, the façade of apparent U.S. military invincibility and political will was slowly eroded. At the same time, the illusion of U.S. economic unimpeachability was also shattered, with the Global Financial Crisis incubated in the United States paralyzing Western economies as China's own less integrated capital markets and rapid fiscal interventions effectively insulated the Chinese economy and acted as a force for global stability during the period of ensuing related crises in Europe and elsewhere. As Washington dithered in the desert and Western economies floundered, the CCP leadership decided that it was time to abandon the policy first articulated by Deng and followed by each subsequent Chinese leader, to "hide our capabilities, keep a low profile, and bide our time."[14] Beijing's opening moves in this regard began with its assertion of a sphere of influence in its immediate vicinity, not dissimilar to, indeed derived directly from, the example of Washington's own assertion of the Monroe Doctrine.[15] While Beijing merely sought effective control over the waters directly adjoining the country, that prompted an immediate and alarmed response from Washington.

Obama's 2011 "pivot," or "rebalancing," to Asia could hardly have been more transparent. While really the CCP was simply seeking to reconcile the difference between its acquired economic and military power with its existing, relatively lowly geopolitical station — in effect becoming what FDR and Truman had envisioned it becoming during the post-World War II period, one of the globe's "four policemen" responsible for maintaining security and economic stability in its region — Washington, high on

---

[14] Fully expressed, Deng's 1990 "24-character strategy" reads: "Observe calmly; secure our position; cope with affairs calmly; hide our capacities and bide our time; be good at maintaining a low profile; and never claim leadership."

[15] In ignoring the 2016 United Nations Permanent Court of Arbitration ruling against China's South China Sea claims, one hears echoes of President Theodore Roosevelt's 1901 quip that "the Monroe Doctrine is not a question of 'law' at all. It is a question of policy."

unipolarity, immediately set about trying to block China's attempts at asserting its prerogatives in Southeast Asia.[16] U.S. policymakers ramped up efforts at alliance-building in Southeast Asia, a region relatively neglected since the end of the first Cold War. At the same time, the U.S. overtly sought to undermine attempts by Beijing to build alternative regional institutions to those constructed by the U.S. during the post-World War II period, such as the Asian Infrastructure Development Bank, while developing new institutional frameworks, like the Trans-Pacific Partnership and Quad, that would exclude Beijing. Along with Washington's support for organizations advocating separation from China, such as the World Uyghur Congress, and the construction of a new Cold War narrative pitting "democracy versus authoritarianism," the Trump administration, filled with China hawks, made the new U.S. policy of weakening and containing China explicit in a series of documents formulated within a year of his taking the White House.[17] This stance has been fully embraced by the Biden administration.

Without irony, it is the United States — which since the end of the first Cold War has invaded multiple countries without UN resolutions, has run a secret network of black site torture facilities, has helped to topple multiple governments, and has killed millions of civilians via economic warfare and covert drone campaigns — that accuses Beijing of threatening global peace and security. CCP planners now rightly believe that if China is to have its proper place at the table, one commensurate with its hard and soft power capabilities, it will have to fight the United States.[18] While it has achieved a great deal and may achieve still more, so far as China's own dreamiest

---

[16] For more on American thinking on the matter, see John Gaddis, *The United States and the Origins of the Cold War* (1972) or Hoopes and Brinkley's *FDR and the Creation of the U.N.* (1997).

[17] These were, in no particular order, the 2017 U.S. National Security Strategy (NSS), the 2018 U.S. National Defense Strategy (NDS), and a 2018 special report from the U.S. Trade Representative (USTR). With the first stating: "For decades U.S. policy was rooted in the belief that support for China's rise and integration would liberalize China, but that this assumption turned out to be false." Instead, China was "a rival." The NDS stated: "Beijing will continue to pursue a military modernization program that seeks Indo-Pacific regional hegemony in the near-term, and displacement of the United States to achieve global preeminence in the future."

[18] Christian Shepherd, "China's Foreign Minister Predicts Impending Clash with the United States," *Washington Post*, March 7, 2023.

aspirations and the worst nightmares of Pentagon planners go, the reality is that China's outlook is relatively limited. For all the talk of China's apparently inevitable rise and route to global domination, a closer look at its internal and external situation leaves significant room for doubt — even about the long-term durability of the Chinese state as presently constituted.

Chapter 3:
China's Internal Problems and
External Constraints

Confronting the arguments of hawks and attempting to persuade those who would be convinced by a dispassionate consideration of the evidence would require one to demonstrate that China is, in fact, not ten feet tall. Sowing doubt about the hawks' narrative, then, is a primary objective of any opponent of the fake China Threat narrative. When it comes to China's power projection capabilities, these doubts can be broken down into five basic categories: geographic impediments, resource constraints, demographic collapse, lack of national cohesion, and economic slowdown.

Geography

China's geography is frankly terrible in terms of potential power projection capability. Internally, it features endless flatlands to the north, abutting deserts and mountains running to the west, with more mountains and dense jungle to the south, while its eastern coast is ringed by states terrified of an expansionist China. More on these states, as well as China's myriad other neighbors to north, south, and west and the various problems they pose to Chinese power projection, later.

But to continue with China's internal problems stemming from its geography, because of its vast population it is seriously strapped for foodstuffs. A shocking statistic: on a per capita basis, it has less arable agricultural land than Saudi Arabia, making the fact that it has long been the world's largest food importer unsurprising.[19] Further, what farmland China does have requires enormous amounts of petrochemical fertilizers and laborers to keep the land even moderately productive. Further, lacking a confluence of natural and traversable, interconnected east-west-flowing waterways, moving mass amounts of produce around internally is expensive and inefficient over the vast distances that locally produced foodstuffs would have to travel in order to get to the highly populated eastern seaboard provinces. Given these facts, as well as others to follow, as presently situated China is arguably the most globalization-dependent state on earth.

---

[19] From: The World Bank, "Arable Land" (see Works Cited).

Resource Constraints

On pace to become the world's largest consumer of oil in coming years, surpassing the United States, China itself holds less than 2 percent of all proven oil reserves.[20] Little wonder that the so-called "Malacca and Hormuz Dilemmas," which could effectively shut down China's entire economy overnight, have long been a central focus of CCP military planners.[21] While it has plenty of coal (the fourth most globally, according to estimates), the already serious amount of environmental degradation wrought by the CCP's policy of breakneck industrialization, resulting in regular protests and serious widespread health problems, would make use of the coal difficult to sustain socially and politically. In terms of natural gas, what little China has lies in the culturally distinct Sichuan and Xinjiang provinces, a potential source of myriad problems that may, along with the advanced technologies required to exploit it effectively, explain Beijing's relative reluctance to embrace its development.[22] Apart from the paucity of high-yield agricultural land, China is also plagued by water scarcity; its solutions, which cost an estimated $100 billion annually, are causing increased desertification and displacement in the parts of the country from which water is being diverted.[23] In an environmental disaster zone lacking many of the basic necessities to sustain its enormous population, any serious disruption to the existing globalized order would likely cause hundreds of millions of Chinese to famish if not literally starve to death.

Demographic Collapse

The CCP's social engineering projects add their own complications to China's already considerable domestic problems. From a combination of more or less forced mass urbanization, state-induced famine, and two-child, then one-child, policies, the CCP faces demographic collapse. Specifically, it is going to run out of taxpayers, laborers, and consumers. Even worse, not only did changing to a one-child policy in the 1980s amplify the severity of the coming crisis, but it led to an epidemic of sex-selective abortion.[24] So

---

[20] Worldometers, "China Oil" (see Works Cited).

[21] You Ji, "Dealing with the Malacca Dilemma: China's Effort to Protect its Energy Supply," Published September 18, 2007, in *Strategic Analysis*.

[22] Worldometers, "China Natural Gas" (see Works Cited).

[23] Amelia Browne, "Desertification in China: Causes, Impacts, and Solutions," Earth.org. Published December 20, 2022.

[24] Hesketh et al., "The Consequences of Son Preference and Sex-Selective

not only does the regime have tens of millions of young men unable to find girlfriends or, increasingly, jobs (more on that later), but by 2030 China will have an estimated four retirees for every two workers and every one newborn.[25]

Two additional things are worth pointing out here. First, while it is true that Xi reversed the CCP's policies, it isn't going to matter because the cost of raising children in China makes having more of them prohibitively expensive, while at the same time urbanization and industrialization naturally decrease birthrates anyway (see every other industrialized and post-industrial country in history). Second, while the surfeit of single young males unable to find jobs or wives is probably U.S. hawks' strongest argument for why China might pose a serious threat to one or more of its neighbors — unable to do anything else with such a potentially dangerous lot, Beijing may decide to throw them into a meatgrinder of a conflict over Taiwan or in another border war with India — their existence poses no danger to the U.S.

Lack of National Cohesion

Apart from the separatists holed up on Taiwan, large populations of Uyghurs and Tibetans inconveniently located in strategic areas far from Beijing, as well as dozens of much smaller ethnic groups in the mountainous jungles to the south, mean that the CCP leadership faces multiple permanent secessionist dangers far from its northeastern core. Further such threats follow directly from the geography of the country, with wealthier eastern coastal provinces such as Jiangsu and Zhejiang wanting and having far more to do with wealthier Japan and Korea and the rest of the outside world than with the hinterlands of China's western barrens. Such provinces have historically resisted Beijing's control, and the CCP's most recent moves against the Shanghai-centered tech sector and its billionaire class ought to be understood in this light;[26] so, too, Beijing's initial hesitance to ape the U.S. shale revolution because of the location of most of China's shale deposits in large, wealthy, and culturally distinct

---

Abortion in China and other Asian Countries," *Canadian Medical Association Journal*. Published September 6, 2011; Volume 183 (12): pp. 1374–77.

[25] Charlie Campbell, "China's Aging Population is a Major Threat to its Future," *Time*, (February 7, 2019).

[26] Interested readers can check out Andrew Colliers, *China's Technology War: Why Beijing Took Down its Tech Giants* (2022).

Sichuan province; while its campaigns against the Uyghurs and Tibetans already receive considerable (if exaggerated) international attention and consequent opprobrium. Though force or the fear of it can keep them all in line, as well as Hong Kong's recently suppressed population, and those within the CCP itself who do not favor Xi's policies, that ability to use force rests on the CCP's claim to legitimacy and its ability to mobilize sufficient resources to police these regions effectively and put down any potential trouble — which is to say its state power.

Economic Slowdown

Since state power ultimately rests on economic power, it is worth appreciating the myriad problems that China's hitherto racing economy faces on both the domestic and foreign fronts.[27] Because of its unique position over the past thirty years as a mass global exporter, the CCP has managed to stave off any potential economic slowdowns with boundless state credit, industry subsidies, and dumping, thereby maintaining near-full employment. However, decreasing returns on additional debt and continued overproduction, combined with domestic underconsumption, and low-cost labor competition in its region and around the world, mean that the bill is about to come due. It's going to be enormous.

As of 2021, China's total debt was three times its annual economic output, and the expansion of debt and credit has accelerated in recent years.[28] Until 2021, the Chinese financial system had for several years previously been increasing its money supply significantly faster than the never-shy Federal Reserve System.[29] Reminiscent of the experience of the United States, the rise of shadow banking in China contributed significantly to this process. Including public and private borrowings, it is possible that as much as $7 trillion in bad debt is hidden away in the opaque Chinese financial system.[30] Further, much of the debt is short-term, meaning that it

---

[27] For book-length treatments readers can consult: Ho-fung Hung, *The China Boom: Why China Will Not Rule the World* (2017); George Magnus, *Red Flags: Why Xi's China Is in Jeopardy* (2018); or Dinny McMahon, *China's Great Wall of Debt: Shadow Banks, Ghost Cities, Massive Loans, and the End of the Chinese Miracle* (2018).

[28] Amanda Lee, "China Debt: Has it Changed in 2021 and How Big Is It Now?" *South China Post,* June 5, 2021.

[29] Trading Economics, "United States Money Supply M2" and "China Money Supply M2" (see Works Cited).

[30] Gabriel Wildau, "Prominent China Debt Bear Warns of $6.8 Trillion in Hidden Losses," *Financial Times,* August 16, 2017; and Bloomberg News, "China's $6

is frequently rolled over with new debt. This ongoing practice is yielding ever-decreasing returns. According to the *Economist*, fully three-quarters of new loans in China simply go toward paying the interest on existing debt. Meanwhile, total factor productivity, which had soared during the first decade of the new century, has flatlined since then — with its 1.4 billion citizens still producing nowhere near what the industrialized Western economies do per capita — and Xi's own insistence on reasserting state control over the private sector, which is responsible for most of the productivity gains over the past two decades, is likely to continue this already worrying trend.

Abroad, the Belt and Road Initiative (BRI) is only making things worse: spawning even more Renminbi (or Yuan), which are lent and spent on projects of questionable economic value and equally dubious means of repayment. Again, however, CCP policies that privilege employment and state stability over efficiency and productivity mean that China's industrial overproduction has to have somewhere to go, even if it means lending to countries like Venezuela, which quickly defaulted, or like Sri Lanka, which when it was forced to sign over its principal port instigated a wave of anti-Chinese sentiment within the country and bad press for so-called "debt-trap development" around the globe. This is to say nothing of problems in places like Pakistan, one of the BRI's key nodes, which has featured repeated setbacks and disturbances, particularly in violently separatist Baluchistan. The project, a geopolitical brainchild of Xi, is now subject to regular, if polite, criticism within Chinese academic and policy circles, with increasing numbers of critics coming to recognize the project for what it is: a boondoggle aimed at increasing Chinese power and influence abroad rather than doing anything to increase the welfare of the still relatively poor Chinese people domestically, whose income per capita is ranked 79th globally.[31]

Though it brought China quickly up the ranks of the developing economies, the CCP's relationship of mutual economic interdependence on the collective West, and the United States in particular, now hangs

---

Trillion Hidden Debt gets Stress-Tested in Downturn," November 17, 2021.

[31] In terms of living standards, on a per capita basis Chinese citizens consume half the meat annually that their American counterparts do, have only half the amount of average square feet of living space, use only half as much electricity, receive about half as much schooling, and have lower life expectancies (see Works Cited).

ominously over its head. The U.S. and China's economic interdependence was part of the strategy of integrating China into the world economy in order to cultivate its passivity toward U.S. prerogatives and further its domestic transformation into a democracy. The latter, of course, failed; and as the relationship deepened, both sides came to recognize that they were now locked into a situation of mutually assured economic destruction — as evidenced by Beijing's unwillingness to pounce on the United States during its prolonged economic crisis just over a decade ago, this despite alleged Russian encouragement to do so.[32]

However, there exists a key asymmetry within the relationship, and every U.S. security strategist knows it: in the event of a massive economic crash, in a democracy there is another election, whereas in an authoritarian state there is likely to be revolution.[33] This danger has been highlighted by the U.S.-coordinated Western response to Russia's invasion of Ukraine in February 2022. China, whose economy is far more tied into world trade, has just seen what a coordinated response from the richer Western nations can do. While Russia will be able to outlast U.S. sanctions by shifting commodity exports to a willing developing world, were a similar situation to occur over Taiwan, China would not have any such outlet for its abundance of manufactured goods, and its internal market, while growing, is still too underdeveloped to absorb the surpluses. Of course, whether or not such a coordinated response would be forthcoming in such an event is another question (as evidence, see Macron's statements made during a visit to China during April 2023).[34]

As though these multi-front domestic problems weren't enough, China has the further misfortune of being surrounded on all sides. A detailed analysis of each of China's fourteen neighbors is not necessary to illustrate the essential difficulty of Beijing's situation. However, a summary of the

---

[32] That comes from the memoir of then-Secretary of the Treasury Hank Paulson.

[33] See the collected case studies edited by Victor C. Shih in *Economic Shocks and Authoritarian Stability* (2020) for an in-depth analysis of evidence from regimes around the globe.

[34] These ran, in part: "The great risk Europe faces is that it gets caught up in crises that are not ours, which prevents it from building its strategic autonomy... The paradox would be that, overcome with panic, we believe we are just America's followers... the question Europeans need to answer is: is it in our interest to accelerate [a crisis] on Taiwan? No. The worse thing would be to think that we Europeans must become followers on this topic and take our cue from the U.S. agenda and a Chinese overreaction."

major players, their domestic incentive structures, and their perception of a rising China as a threat to their own security and wider interests is vital to understanding why China is unlikely to attain even regional hegemony regardless of Washington's own (redundant and dangerous) policies aimed at preventing that outcome.

India: Washington, beginning with George W. Bush, set out to cultivate India, despite its history of non-alignment, as a future balancer against China. Creating the so-called "123 Agreement," a legal loophole that allowed Delhi to proceed with its nuclear program without fear of U.S. sanctions, Washington simultaneously played on Indian fears of Pakistan and its relationship with China. Not eager to be seen overtly choosing sides, Delhi mostly kept its head down through the 2000s, focusing on growing India's economy, military, and overall state power. In the 2010s, Beijing's growing assertiveness pushed Delhi — who never does anything contrary to its own perceived interests, whatever Washington might prefer — into embracing Washington's increasingly overt attempts to contain China and ultimately into joining the re-formed Quad in 2017. A series of standoffs over disputed regions on the border between China and India finally erupted in a series of skirmishes between Chinese and Indian troops in 2020. These were a "turning point," according to Nirupama Rao, India's former Foreign Secretary and Ambassador to both the United States and China, prompting realization that the possibility of 1960s-style full-out conflict between the two was indeed a distinct possibility. Considering how India now has a population larger than that of China, an economy already the fifth largest in the world as measured by GDP, and a geography ideal for power projection in the Indian Ocean, with a growing naval power to match, China's loss of India to the side of the growing balancing coalition was huge and totally self-inflicted.

Japan: along with India, Japan was the most significant of China's neighbors never likely to partake in bandwagoning with a rising China. The historical animosities, both ancient and recent, are deep, and Japan's capacities to resist, like India's, were too considerable to make that a desirable or palatable option. Still the third largest economy in the world despite decades of government mismanagement, Japan has long had the ability to remilitarize quickly and even to nuclearize, the latter likely within the span of months rather than years. Like Delhi, Tokyo has outstanding border disputes with China, particularly over the Senkaku/Diaoyu Dao

Islands, and was one of the first to sound the alarm over growing Chinese assertiveness in the South and East China Seas. Unlike India, whose vital natural resource imports would not even be threatened by Chinese regional hegemony given its open access to the Indian Ocean and Middle East, under such conditions Japan could find itself on the receiving end of a Malacca Straits-style dilemma. Home to multiple U.S. Army and Navy installations, and playing host to nearly 60,000 U.S. troops, Tokyo is happy to foot the bill for anyone who wants to contain China — with the hawkish and powerful Shinzo Abe quietly and not so quietly shaping policy behind the scenes until his bizarre assassination in 2022.

The Philippines: yet another neighbor with outstanding border disputes with Beijing, Manila isn't eager for confrontation with China but recognizes that its own strategic interests are threatened by its increasingly assertive larger neighbor. If there was any doubt following the confrontation over the Scarborough Shoals in 2012, this was made clear when Beijing waved aside the Permanent Court of Arbitration's 2016 ruling in Manila's favor over the issue of China's so-called "nine-dash line." Even Rodrigo Duterte, who came to office openly pursuing partnership with Beijing, eventually backtracked and reverted to the side of the growing balancing coalition, moving to restore prior defense agreements, supporting AUKUS, and expanding joint military exercises (while his successor, Ferdinand Marcos, Jr., reopened bases for the U.S. Navy). Again, this was largely the product of Chinese belligerence over disputed islands and reefs, as well as under-delivery on Chinese promises of the economic benefits that would flow to the Philippines were it to align with Beijing. Along with Japan, Taiwan, Brunei, Indonesia, and Malaysia, the Philippines forms part of a dense thicket impeding Chinese access to the Pacific and Indian Oceans. While still dwarfed by China economically, and alone would stand no chance against China in an economic or kinetic conflict, together these countries have a larger population to draw from, considerable resources, and not irrelevant economic heft, while their disparate thousands of islands and jungle geographies make the idea of an all-out military campaign against them an all but laughable hypothetical endeavor.

South Korea: Seoul's interest in balancing against a rising China is perhaps the most obvious of any state detailed thus far. Its own territorial dispute with Beijing is relatively negligible (that of Socotra Rock), but the Democratic People's Republic of Korea, its highly militarized northerly neighbor, with its million-man army, nuclear weapons, and backing by China, looks formidable. And, of course, the war between North and South is still technically ongoing, as no war-ending treaty was ever signed. Like the territory of modern Vietnam, the Korean Peninsula was also for centuries part of the Chinese sphere of influence. South Korea's interests, therefore, while complicated like everyone else's in the region through economic ties with China, are solidly on the side of any balancing coalition. Were one not to form, a scenario rather unlikely given the incentives of the other major states already detailed, it is conceivable that Seoul would turn to Beijing for protection from Pyongyang. But in terms of its values, economy, politics, and world outlook, it is solidly opposed to Chinese regional hegemony. With the tenth largest economy in the world, South Korea brings a rich consumer market, loads of cutting-edge industry, and a strategic location to a balancing coalition, with the possibility of basing to any allies on offer to go with its own growing blue-water navy, already eighth largest in the world in total tonnage.

Summary: while their interests often conflict in many areas, from trade to natural resource rights to human rights, on the issue of balancing against Beijing the interests of each of the above governments, as well as those of Vietnam, Australia, Malaysia, and Indonesia (to say nothing of Taiwan), almost perfectly coincide, though it should be noted that governments are not their populations, and further that real differences exist between factions within these various political structures (see Australian Labor's newfound opposition to AUKUS). Meanwhile, those of China's neighbors variously willing to brook increasing Chinese dominance, such as Cambodia, Myanmar, and Thailand, are unreliable, impoverished, and in each case suffering multiple armed insurgencies and secessionist groups that receive various levels of outside aid. Coupled with China's own internal problems already outlined, China's daunting perimeter of rival states means that the threat of Chinese regional hegemony is a distant, if totally unrealizable, prospect. While the disappearance of the U.S. military from the region would certainly change the dynamics between states, there is little reason to think that balancing against China would not occur, or that Beijing would suddenly start ordering invasions of all its neighbors. Apart from the likely costs and consequences of such decisions, these are some of its best customers. Further, even if it were true that Beijing were intent on fighting its neighbors, if they can't adequately defend themselves, why should the United States get involved? All such academic analyses of China's internal and external environment aside, why should Washington, D.C., be the arbiter of what goes on in East Asia? Because our parents, grandparents, or great-grandparents fought multiple unnecessary wars there almost a century ago under false pretenses and in the name of a grandiose imperial vision no longer sustainable?

Bottom line: even if one accepts the flawed logic of Great Power competition, courting conflict with Beijing is foolish of Washington. For either China really is as strong as D.C. and its loyal corporate mouthpieces claim, in which case antagonizing China over issues directly in its backyard is stupid; or China is actually quite weak, in which case antagonizing China in its backyard is unnecessary and counterproductive. After all, it is worth noting that fragmentation rather than unity has defined Chinese history. Spanning approximately two millennia, for only three hundred of those years were the borders of today's China united, more or less, under a Han-dominated central political authority. Left to itself, locked in the South and East China Seas, it seems as plausible that China could face the threat of serious collapse and fragmentation by the late 2030s as it does anything else.

In any event, it is hard to imagine how the life of the average American would be improved by courting conflict with China, while it is quite easy to imagine countless ways in which it could be made worse. Americans can and should say "No!" to Cold War 2.0. It is not only ethically indefensible but materially and strategically unnecessary and dangerous. Far from being one hundred feet tall, China is just an ordinary state with approximately proportional power projection capabilities for its economy, size, and demography. Everything else is in Washington's head. And, as intelligent observers have noted, particularly in the last year, the harder Washington pushes, the more it undermines its own relative position and strengthens that of Beijing. Unsurprisingly to critics of government policy generally, virtually everything D.C. does is counterproductive to its stated goal of containing China, much like how the last twenty years of war in the Middle East were meant to undermine Iran but ultimately left it strategically stronger than before. Again, though, it is incumbent upon the American people to say "No" to this behavior, because all incentive structures in Washington have evolved in such a way that the most likely outcome will continue to be decisions contrary to the peace and prosperity of the American people.

Chapter 4:
China as a Global Player

Naturally, having more or less run the world for the past generation, and having been one of the only two decisive global actors for fifty years prior to that, Washington views any activities by China anywhere in the world as uniformly coordinated and nefarious attempts at undermining its position and preferred policies. Even when it comes to building hospitals, roads, or bridges in Africa, the hawks in D.C. can be counted on to disparage or dismiss such activities as mere pretense or "debt-trap" diplomacy. Such narcissism and projection aside, the reality is that China is a global player; and while the Renminbi is not likely ever to be the world reserve currency, nor is Beijing ever likely to enjoy a globe-spanning military presence of some 800 bases, China's ability to exert its power and influence is likely to increase in the coming years. So far, despite some definitely aggressive posturing where its immediate interests are concerned, as in the South China Sea, China's exertions have resulted in virtually no bloodshed and no wars in over forty years. Not that such metrics matter to Washington; what matters in D.C. is that Beijing uphold the "rules-based international order" on terms strictly acceptable to it. As an example of what this looks like in point of practice, take the recent peace deal between Iran and Saudi Arabia brokered by China (probably, but not necessarily, with some behind-the-scenes help from ally and fellow BRICS member Russia).

Those who have followed the background noise of U.S. activities in the Middle East over the past year, since it was last seriously in the news following the disastrous execution by the Biden administration of the long overdue withdrawal from Afghanistan, will recall a vague haze of reported drone strikes, arms sales, and Israeli assassinations; more recently, they will recall resistance to attempts to end the U.S. military roles in Syria and Yemen, the death of the Iran nuclear deal, and the blocking of earthquake relief in Syria. China, by contrast, with no military presence in the Middle East at all, quietly concluded talks between the Iranian and Saudi leadership that resulted in the normalizing of their diplomatic relations. Quite the contrast. And despite complaints by the hawks and Israel-Firsters in the Democratic and Republican Parties, this deal is good for multiple reasons. First, it will help end the wars in Yemen and Syria where Iran and Saudi Arabia have been among the chief backers of opposite sides of the proxy conflicts. Together, they've gone on for over twenty years and killed hundreds of thousands of people. Further, this deal signals that China, who buys most of the oil from the Gulf monarchies these days, is going to start more actively investing political capital in the region. As the only party that can be trusted by all sides concerned, Beijing is ideally situated to mediate the invariably arising disputes. There are real costs involved in this, and it would be good to see someone other than the American taxpayer start footing these bills.[35]

Here we find all the elements of the above-described dynamics, where Washington acts like anything that happens anywhere without its imprimatur constitutes a threat to national security. One is reminded of Ted Cruz recently embarrassing himself by claiming the same about the mere temporary docking of two small Iranian warships in Brazil. Worth noting as an aside, their permission to dock came despite months of reported pressure from Washington to deny them port and after Lula had already been to Washington to meet with Biden. Apart from knowing that somewhere at the State Department someone is being paid a six-figure salary to harass Brazilian officials for *literal months* about a pair of small Iranian vessels taking port in their ostensibly independent and sovereign country, everywhere everyone seems to be taking every opportunity to try to send Washington the message that they have no interest in yet another round of so-called "Great Power" competition.

In short, China's facilitation of these talks between Iran and Saudi Arabia was a good thing to see. It will help bring peace and save lives. Or, as State Department shill Jonathan Panikoff, writing for the Atlantic Council, put it: "It should be a warning to U.S. policymakers: Leave the Middle East and abandon ties with frustrating, even barbarous, but long-standing allies, and you'll simply be leaving a vacuum for China to fill." Fill

---

[35] Really the only conceivable potential downside to the deal being done between Riyadh and Tehran is that it may complicate efforts to normalize Saudi-Israeli relations. But here it should be noted that any potential deal to get that done already looks terrible from the point of view of the average American: Riyadh's demands include formal American security guarantees, more weapons, and a nuclear program. Realistically, given the power of the Israel lobby, Washington's failed policy of wasting American lives and treasure in pursuit of Israeli policy priorities in the Middle East hardly looks likely to be seriously disturbed by China's mediation of Riyadh and Tehran's most recent spat. If it is going to be disturbed by anything, it will be by the new Israeli government. But that is another story.

with what? Peace? To replace four decades of Washington's wars? The horror!

Chapter 5:
Chinese Foreign Policy Historically

An examination of Chinese foreign policy historically lends little support to those who depict China as secretly plotting to take over the world. Rather, it points to an entity preoccupied with managing its complex local strategic environment and internal security concerns. While no single, brief section devoted to the subject could comprehensively make such a case in detail, a few general observations are worth pointing out for their relation to the present. For despite what proponents of the New Red Scare would have us believe, China and its nominally Communist leadership have for decades acted in a way that is strictly nationalist ideologically. It is therefore important to understand what, to borrow Palmerston's phrase, China's eternal interests are and how they have been pursued.

A Few Thousand Years of Chinese Foreign Policy in a Nutshell

Surrounded on virtually all sides, the history of Chinese foreign policy is one of permanent flux, of an ever-changing external security environment made more complex by the actually quite heterogeneous makeup of the peoples and lands that have historically constituted the core of China. For, of course, with the nation state being a relatively modern creation of the Europeans, globalized during the Age of Empire and its aftermath, "China" existed less as a specific geographical entity than as a cultural entity, a civilization rather than a state, to borrow from the American political scientist and Sinologist Lucian Pye.

That civilization had at its core the Han of the Yellow River valley, Confucianism, and under the later Sui (581–618), Tang (618–906), and Song (960–1279) dynasties the formalization of a meritocratic bureaucracy filled by way of a civil service examination to run the Imperial system. Its elite being centralized and bureaucratic rather than decentralized and militaristic, while this reduced the tendency of earlier periods toward fragmentation under competing warlords, made China vulnerable to attack by the many surrounding "barbarians" (i.e., non-Sinicized people).

One common solution to this problem was, to quote the Chinese-American Sinologist Yang Lien-sheng, "using barbarians to check barbarians" or "using barbarians to fight barbarians."[36] When this failed, however, conquering barbarians were often effectively Sinicized as easily as though it were they who had been conquered and not the other way around. The Mongol Yuan (1279–1368) and Manchu Qing (1644–1911) dynasties were examples of this reverse assimilation, undergone by the new ruling class as a way to ensure their effective control over a vast and complex territory.

While the Chinese state did, over the course of its thousands of years of history and multitudinous dynasties and instantiations, go through local periods of expansion via conquest[37] or colonization, the geographical difficulties, costliness, and uncertainties of attempting to project and sustain concentrated military power on so many fronts meant that the favored Chinese order was one which saw China as central but by no means all-encompassing or even truly hegemonic. While its cultural and economic influence in East Asia was significant, and its view of itself as the center of civilization was understandable given its preponderance, material wealth, and technological superiority, China's foreign policy generally was not concerned with expanding its trade, culture, or territorial reach much beyond its immediate environs, and the existence of independent kingdoms in places like Japan and Vietnam were long-established facts.

The Century of Humiliation

With China's attention focused inward, external trade largely eschewed, and advances in military and naval affairs either unpursued or abandoned, when the Western powers first began more assertively to try and open up China in the 19th century, seeking trading concessions, privileges for their nationals, and permanent diplomatic presences, the reaction of the Imperial government was to attempt to follow the time-tested template of using barbarians to fight barbarians by inviting in a variety of barbarians, like the French, Americans and Russians, so that they might fight with one another and thereby become weak enough that they might all be ejected.

---

[36] Yang Lien-sheng, "Historical Notes on the Chinese World Order" from *The Chinese World Order: Traditional China's Foreign Relations* (Published by Harvard University Press, 1968).

[37] Arguably the single most important period of such expansion and state building occurred during the 18th century, when the aforementioned Manchu Qing dynasty expanded China's territorial reach to its greatest extent via a series of campaigns into Central and Southeast Asia under the Qianlong Emperor (1735–1796).

This, of course, did not happen, as the ambition of these barbarians was not to conquer and rule China but to extract resources from it. Far from eager to see the Imperial government in Beijing fall, the Western powers helped to prop it up, understanding like the Manchu and Mongols before them that the vastness and complexity of the empire required a military and bureaucratic capacity beyond any of them. Despite their efforts, however, the losses to Great Britain and its allies in the Opium Wars (1839–42 and 1856–60) and their consequent "unequal treaties" sparked off multiple internal rebellions (1850–64, 1851–68, 1856–72, 1862–67, 1895–96, and 1899–1901) as Imperial legitimacy was tainted and central authority weakened.

The dawning of the 20th century saw Revolution (1911–12), betrayal by their Western allies at Versailles (1919), warlord-ism (1916–28), invasion by Japan (1931), the Second Sino-Japanese War (1937–45), and concurrent Civil War (1927–49). In short, the so-called "Century of Humiliation" (1839–1949) saw a China unable to act independently; and it was not until the eventual triumph of Mao's Chinese Communist Party that China began, in his words, to "stand up."

Standing Up

Western observers were surprisingly slow to recognize the ideological significance of the communist states fighting with one another: particularism, not universalism, was to be communism's defining feature. (Note: even earlier it should have been telling that Stalin, to muster support for war against the Nazis, had called on Russian patriotism, not Marxist doctrine.)

Historical memory, as well as Stalin's own hard-driving realism in his negotiations with Mao, meant that Sino-Soviet relations were always going to be precarious rather than fraternal. And when Khruschev turned on Stalin after the dictator's death, Mao used the opportunity to assert China's definite autonomy, denying the Soviets access to Chinese territory and eschewing cooperation. Competing for influence in the various revolutionary hotspots abroad further soured relations, as did Soviet backing for India.

Mao's eventual decision to try opening to the United States, therefore, was prompted by the long-term deterioration in Sino-Soviet relations as well as a recognition of China's national strategic interests.[38] And as war with the Soviet Union became increasingly likely in the late 1960s, Mao sought an opening on the basis of a classical strategy of Chinese history: engaging the far enemy while fighting the near.

Engagement with the United States had the additional benefit of helping make China rich again; and especially with the disappearance of a common foe and the immediate examples of U.S. military unilateralism in the 1990s, Chinese leaders began to use China's newfound wealth and technological capabilities to harness an "anti-access/area denial" strategy to protect and preserve its regained autonomy, a capability it lacked for centuries and which in effect made the South China Sea into a Western lake.

A policy of "full-spectrum dominance" this is not. Rather, Beijing has sought to defend China's long-standing interests by finding ways to push back asymmetrically against the often superior conventional forces deployed against them.[39]

Conclusion

It seems incredible, more than thirty years after the fall of the Soviet Union and decades after the Chinese embraced state capitalism, that anyone would fall for the obvious and worn tropes of the dangers of "communists" taking over the world. And yet each day millions of Americans now tune in to lurid descriptions of the allegedly perfidious activities not of "Beijing," "Xi," or "China," but of the *Chinese Communist Party.*

But this is nonsense. Xi rouses the population with nationalist talk, not Marxist or Maoist talking points. National pride aside, he and his cronies are interested in enriching themselves and being in power, and much like being a member of the Republican or Democratic Party in the United States is required to loot the country effectively, so, too, is it required that in China one be a member of its official governing party.

As Samuel Huntington observed in 1996, a reconstituted and powerful China interested in resurrecting its classical sphere of influence was already a "cultural and economic reality" in the process of becoming "a political one." Tellingly, he went on to predict: "The dangerous clashes of the future are likely to arise from the interaction of Western arrogance... and Sinic

---

[38] For a comprehensive analysis of the Sino-Soviet split, see Danhui Li and Xafeng Xia *Mao and the Sino-Soviet Split, 1959–1973: A New History* (2020).

[39] An interesting, oft-cited work in this regard comes from a pair of PLA officers, Qiao Liang and Wang Xiangsui, *Unrestricted Warfare* (1999).

assertiveness… What is universalism to the West is imperialism to the rest."[40]

This prescience aside, if FDR could cut deals with Stalin, and Nixon could sit down with Mao, then Joe Biden or Donald Trump should be able to get along with the likes of Xi (or Putin for that matter), lest a clash of civilizations end civilization entirely.

---

[40] Quotes from Huntington's *The Clash of Civilizations and the Remaking of World Order* (1998), pp. 169, 183–4.

Chapter 6:
What the Heck is a "Scarborough Shoal" and China's (other) Territorial Disputes

News from Southeast Asia during the fall of 2023 featured repeated reports of the Biden administration rattling its saber over incidents between the Philippines and China in the South China Sea.[41] At issue are some spits of sand thousands of miles from the United States. Just as a refresher for those Americans who, rightly, have no idea what or where the Scarborough or Second Thomas Shoal are (so irrelevant are they to American prosperity or security) ...

The origins of the dispute between China and the Philippines over these miniscule spits of land in the South China Sea are based on conflicting claims over the territory. Beijing's are based on ancient maps and documents it believes prove its sovereignty over the area, the so-called nine-dash line; while Manila, for its part, points to treaties and agreements signed during the colonial period when the Philippines was under Spanish and then American rule—among them, the 1898 Treaty of Paris and subsequently formulated Constitution of the Philippines, both of which included the shoals. Apart from being strategically located between China and the Philippines, they are home to rich fisheries and are likely to have significant reserves of oil and gas within their exclusive economic zone. As such, it is understandable why both Beijing and Manila are reluctant to concede their claims, and despite numerous efforts at doing so over the years, no resolution between the two has ever been reached.

Seeking to defend and strengthen its claim with a permanent armed presence, in 1999 Manila ordered the *Sierra Madre* purposefully run aground on Second Thomas Shoal, leaving the ship and a small contingent of men who are

---

[41] Gomez and Mistreanu (2023). "US renews warning it will defend Philippines after incidents with Chinese Vessels in South China Sea," Associated Press, October 23.

occasionally resupplied. It was actually attempted Chinese interference in such a resupply effort that sparked the most recent confrontation that the Biden administration issued its warning over. Such incidents have been happening regularly since 2012, when Beijing began sending maritime surveillance vessels and large numbers of Chinese fisherman and members of its merchant marine into the area. When Manila attempted to arrest the Chinese for illegal fishing off Scarborough Shoal, Beijing dispatched more ships to block them, and a standoff ensued that was only brought to an end when the Philippines finally recalled its forces. Manila brought the dispute before the Permanent Court of Arbitration the next year, challenging the validity of China's nine-dash line claim. And in 2016 the Court ruled in favor of the Philippines.

As one might expect, Beijing ignored this and has continued to assert its territorial claims with ever more vigor in the ensuing years. Incidents from the deployment of water cannons and laser lights to near collisions have been unfortunately frequent in the years since. And whereas under previous administrations Washington had been reluctant to explicitly state that the 1951 Mutual Defense Treaty between the United States and the Philippines applied to the disputed maritime areas in question, the Donald Trump administration sought to make these explicit during a 2019 visit by then-Secretary of State Mike Pompeo.[42] At the time, the skeptical Duterte administration in Manila kept aloof. Unfortunately, the newly elected boss in Manila is Ferdinand Marcos Jr., son of long-time U.S. sock-puppet dictator Ferdinand Marcos. He has shown no such reluctance to go along with Washinton's preferred policy of all out confrontation with China, going so far as to open new leases to U.S. naval assets in the Cagayan Province, located directly across from Taiwan.[43]

---

[42] Panda, Ankit (2019). "In Philippines, Pompeo Offers Major Alliance Assurance on South China Sea," *The Diplomat*.

[43] Dress, Brad (2023). "Here's where U.S. military will open bases in the Philippines in move to counter China," *The Hill*, April 3.

Despite what the cheerleaders at outlets like the *Washington Post* or *New York Times* would have you believe, this is all completely crazy, and not at all defensive. Risk war with China over a couple piles of rock and sand so the Philippines can have some extra gas and oil, and the U.S. Navy can shove more assets in China's face in preparation for the desired war over a breakaway province of China which Washington already officially acknowledges as part of China?

Come on.

The truth is this standoff between the Philippines and China is part of much larger, ongoing territorial disputes in the South and East China Seas, which involve multiple countries besides China and Philippines; for example, Vietnam, Malaysia, Brunei, and Taiwan, all of them want a taste of the likely natural resource wealth beneath the ocean's floor, as well as the perceived security that comes from controlling the waters nearby.

There is probably going to be some amount of conflict.

The United States should not get involved.

***

Having covered China's ongoing territorial dispute with the Philippines, further details of China's existing, and settled, territorial disputes seemed in order. For not only has Washington explicitly committed Americans to fight and die over several of these disputes, as in the cases of the Philippines and Japan, but understanding their wider context does much to inform and dispel the fake China threat narrative of a red wave poised to wash mercilessly over its weaker neighbors.

We'll start with Japan. Like the dispute between China and the Philippines over the Spratly Islands or Scarborough Shoal, the origins of China's dispute with Japan over the Senkaku or Diaoyu Islands stretch back over a century, and their claims are rooted in differing interpretations of vaguely worded treaties and conflicting historical accounts. Really, though, as then-Premier Zhou Enlai bluntly stated, it was the question of potential undersea oil reserves that made sovereignty over the islands worth disputing. And once the United States, which had been administering the territories in question since the end of World War II, gave up its administrative role, both Tokyo and Beijing got back to disputing possession between them.

For decades Washington took no part. From 2012 to 2014, however, as part of its pivot to Asia, the Barack Obama administration worked with the government of the late Japanese Prime Minister Shinzo Abe to clarify that the United States' 1960 mutual defense treaty obligations pertained to Japan's claimed maritime possessions. As in the Philippines, then, Washington has deliberately expanded the possibility of direct conflict between the United States and China.

Meanwhile, while New Delhi and Beijing have several areas of overlapping territorial claims along their 2,000 mile border, the most contentious of these is in Ladakh, in the mountains and on the Depsang Plains. A short, ferocious war between India and China in 1962 established the present status quo, but things have been far from quiet. In 2020-2021 a series of melees resulted in deaths on both sides. Despite this, the most recent statements from both sides consist of pledges to maintain "peace and tranquility" along their shared border. This is well, because while Washington has no mutual defense treaty with India, it has formed an increasingly close security partnership. And the more adversarial relations between Beijing and New Delhi are perceived to be the more empowered to pursue its containment strategy Washington will feel.

Lastly, the complicated case of Vietnam. Like Japan and the Philippines, Hanoi's disputes with Beijing are entirely maritime in nature. Like India, however, Vietnam shares a land border with its larger neighbor and has fought a relatively recent war against China, that in 1979. But then, like several of China's smaller and less developed neighbors, Vietnam's concern for the preservation of its sovereignty and autonomy have to be carefully balanced with its critical economic relations with Beijing. Indeed, the crux of the dispute between the two has to do almost exclusively with the economic benefits to be derived from sovereignty over the disputed islands in question; the Paracels and Spratly among them. While Hanoi is unlikely ever to be in Washington's pocket, its apprehension over Beijing's assertion of its privileges under the so-called "nine-dash line" means it will welcome Washington's conduct of so-called "freedom of navigation" exercises in these disputed waters. Sailing U.S. warships into waters claimed by China and near its shores in the name of securing oil and fishing rights for Vietnam may not sound like it's in the interest of America or Americans—but hey, that's why you're not in Washington making these decisions.

Despite its almost uniformly cartoonish depiction in the western corporate media as aggressively seeking to bestride the globe, and for all its outstanding border disputes, Beijing has already peacefully settled several such similar long-standing disputes with Kazakhstan, Kyrgyzstan, Tajikistan, Russia, Mongolia, the two Koreas, Laos, Myanmar, and Pakistan. In many of these cases, such as the Koreas, Tajikistan, and Kazakhstan, China accepted a far smaller portion of the territory for itself in the final settlement. In several others, such as the smaller states along its south and southwest, Beijing was equally generous in the terms it accepted.

Make no mistake: this was not because China or its leaders are "generous." Rather, the logic of China's position dictated its policies. Relations with Mongolia, for example, need be nothing but normal, for as things stand Mongolia is effectively an economic colony of China. In the cases of Laos and Myanmar, failure to pursue peaceful settlements on terms acceptable to its neighbors could have caused headaches for Beijing among its many potentially resistive minorities along its long, jungled frontier.

Finally, it is worth pointing out that the government in Taipei, Taiwan, also lays claim to many of the above disputed territories—including several that Beijing has already negotiated away. Further, that it was Chiang's Republic of China that first produced the modern "nine dash line" map laying claim to sovereignty over the South and East China Seas—so the idea that a democratically transformed China would have been some peaceful, pliant good neighbor is oh so much more of Washington's predictable balderdash.

As Joe Biden prepares to meet with Xi Jinping this week, we can only hope that more sensible heads will prevail when it comes to relations with China. The relationship need not be that of best friends, but that does not and should not mean that China is cast in the role of foe instead. Azerbaijan faces no consequences for its recent conquest, nor Egypt for its long and paltry human rights record. Washington needs some grownups at the wheel, ones who will deal pragmatically with the world as it is, not as they envision forcing it to be.

Chapter 7:
The Media and the Fake China Threat

Like Washington's predictably negative reaction to China's peacemaking efforts in the Middle East, the superstructural position of the corporate media makes forecasting their responses to events relating to China equally pedestrian. While one could choose any number of examples to illustrate this, one of the most telling occurred early in 2023 and stands out singularly in just how out of touch with reality the corporate media was and how impoverished editorial standards have become: the "Chinese Spy Balloon."

As readers will no doubt recall, in January 2023 a data-gathering balloon of Chinese origin passed over the continental United States. According to the Pentagon, it was not the first: per a spokesperson, China has launched some two dozen over the past five years, several of which passed over either Florida, Texas, or Guam during that time.[44] Far from being cause for alarm, however, the Pentagon initially reported that "their signals collection ability isn't radically different from other systems available to the Chinese," and that it did not pose "a significantly enhanced threat." In other words, though that particular balloon passed over several sensitive military installations in the central United States, it wasn't as though the Chinese likely learned anything additional of interest — if, in fact, that was even their intention. For their part, Beijing claimed that it was an off-course weather balloon with "limited" maneuverability — something later grudgingly reported by the *Washington Post* (though this was well after the fact). With Beijing calling the incident an "accident" and case of *force majeure*, the stage seemed set for a simple apology.

That was on the Tuesday of that week. By Wednesday, with the fake China Threat live on every channel, it was clear that de-escalating the situation wasn't on the table, just as in 2001, when a U.S. spy plane collided with an intercepting Chinese jet, resulting in the death of the Chinese pilot, over airspace off Hainan Island — airspace which China claimed was its own but which the U.S. contested was international.

---

[44] This and the following can all be found in a variety of *Washington Post* articles from around that time, including the February 4, 2023, opinion piece "The Inside Story of How the U.S. Shot Down the Chinese Balloon," written by Pentagon and CIA spokesperson David Ignatius.

The media talked of little else the rest of the week, while Republicans, ignoring that the Pentagon had declined to shoot the balloon down over Idaho for fear of damage caused by falling debris, took to the lowest fear-mongering imaginable. From Rubio to McCarthy, J.D. Vance to Marjorie Taylor Greene, Trump, and DeSantis, none could get out quickly or emphatically enough just how much of a threat China was and how weak Biden was for not acting completely belligerent about what *might* have been a surveillance balloon, and which, in any case, had *no* extraordinary capabilities and posed *no threat*. Not that facticity had any bearing on coverage of the event; evidentiary standards predictably went out the window as the most irresponsible and baseless speculations were given platform. EMP, nanobots, poison gas — one was reminded of the scaremongering in the runup to the Second Iraq War, when equally fatuous stories of Saddam using drones to attack the United States with anthrax were given a serious platform. But, of course, Biden caved in, turning what could have been a minor incident into an escalating diplomatic spat at a moment when Sino-American relations have scarcely been worse.

Because Washington and Beijing do so much overhead surveillance of one another, this incident, intentional or not, could have gone on to form a platform for dialogue ahead of Blinken's (now canceled) visit to Beijing. Yet rather than taking the opportunity to discuss the important norms of overhead surveillance, the Biden administration caved to domestic political pressure, canceling what would have been the first-ever face-to-face meeting between Xi and a Cabinet-level member of the Biden administration.[45] Biden's final decision to shoot down the admittedly harmless balloon (leaving China to observe goings-on in the United States from their many equally effective low-orbiting surveillance satellites), squandered any potential opportunity for diplomatic settlement. Indeed, after a muted week Beijing responded to the final downing of the balloon by missile off the Carolina coast by threatening to act accordingly under similar circumstances.

---

[45] Though he did cancel, by June Blinken was in China. And while the meeting was mostly unproductive, rather than rattling the saber Blinken issued a statement confirming the One China Policy, based on the Taiwan Relations Act, Three Communiques, and the Six Assurances. Predictably, this rote recitation of long-standing U.S. policy was met with screams of displeasure by the hawks in D.C., especially Republicans, as well as by the corporate press.

Obviously, there are a lot of questions, but even just considering what is known it seems clear that the reason-distorting fake China Threat caused Washington to ignore better options in favor of one to sate a riled-up domestic audience. Making matters worse, the Biden administration has further attempted to spin the retrieval of what remained of the balloon as a major intelligence coup while the U.S. House followed up with a rare unanimous resolution condemning the "brazen violation" of U.S. sovereignty. Piling aboard, the Pentagon changed its tune: as reported in the *Washington Post*, the balloon was transformed overnight into "part of [a] vast aerial surveillance program."[46] With every general or admiral with any stars taking his turn on Capitol Hill these days breathlessly issuing warnings about impending war with China over Taiwan, one is only surprised by how reservedly the Pentagon had acted in the earlier part of that week. Setting aside any questions of why trillions of dollars in defense spending to protect against (much faster moving) incoming flying objects could be credibly deemed inadequate to bring down a slow-moving hot air balloon safely over some of the least densely populated spaces of the industrialized world, a libertarian realist reading of the situation would be that the Pentagon was quite content to see the admittedly harmless airship float in clear view over the country for a week in order to stoke the predictable, mindless media frenzy.

Lost in all of this is the question of whether, had the Biden administration ignored the hawks and publicly taken Beijing at face value, Beijing would have welcomed the opportunity to close the matter with a formal apology. While the *Wall Street Journal* did (briefly) mention that the incident may have been in response to recent so-called "freedom of navigation acts" by the U.S. Navy and its allies through disputed waters claimed by China — and indeed Xi has been under pressure from China's own hawks over what they view as his timidity in response to repeated visits by high-level U.S. delegations to Taiwan — Xi has been recently preoccupied with trying to reassure and woo Western investors and businesses. With supply chain issues and extended arbitrary lockdowns having already prompted major shifts by multinational corporations away from China, rapidly deteriorating relations between Washington and Beijing are further elevating concerns. Considering his need to address these

---

[46] Nakashima et al., "Chinese Balloon Part of Vast Aerial Surveillance Program, U.S. Says," *Washington Post*, February 7, 2023.

concerns, to say nothing of managing his myriad domestic difficulties, it is hard to imagine, particularly given what has been stated publicly, that Xi purposefully ruined his own sit-down with Blinken. Again, although it is possible that he did, or that rogue hawks within the Chinese establishment manufactured the incident in order to sabotage Xi's upcoming meeting with Blinken to prevent any potential détente, the observable facts just seem to militate against it — for example, Xi had already earlier in the week made the gesture of firing the head of China's Weather Service, the agency ostensibly responsible for what Beijing has steadfastly maintained was a weather balloon thrown off course. Of course, not knowing how maneuverable the balloon was, it is hard to assess the credibility of Beijing's claims that it took the flight path it did more or less by accident. And while we might never have learned that piece of information, at least superficially engaging in good-faith dialogue with Beijing over the incident would have put the ball back in Xi's court, affording an opportunity to observe Beijing's calculations, and avoiding the unnecessary worsening of relations between Washington and Beijing that resulted instead.

Beyond any potential tit-for-tat retaliation on the part of Beijing for Washington's response, and the missed opportunity for constructive engagement over surveillance norms, what is most alarming about the situation is the ease with which such a level of public hysteria was manufactured by the corporate media and political elite. Even worse to consider: Is this what they want? Is this being done to foster a thought-climate more permissive of a military response to any potential move by Beijing against Taiwan? The time is now to speak out against any potential changes to the status quo policy vis-à-vis Taiwan. Already the One China policy has been seriously eroded without any public debate, and much more serious changes were nearly smuggled into the 2023 National Defense Authorization Act. We have come to a dangerous place. It was by choice. We could and should choose otherwise, but this requires pushing back against the concerted efforts of those who would see American blood and treasure wasted 5,000 miles from our shores over issues that were effectively decided years ago, and which, if diplomacy fails and they are decided by force of arms, will have terrible consequences for all involved.[47]

---

[47] Fully five months later, the Pentagon finally admitted that the so-called Chinese "Spy Balloon" did not in fact collect any data over the United States at all, as reported by Reuters on June 29, 2023.

Chapter 8:
Hacks, Chips, and Conflicts of Interest

Among the most increasingly ubiquitous offerings in the fake China Threat genre of tepid, pseudo-intellectual scribbling are those devoted to using anecdotes and hypothetical worst-case scenarios to convince Americans that, while they may be safe from conventional attack, the frontier of new, future, or even existing technologies render them all but helpless in the face of blatant, though somehow still surreptitious, Chinese evildoing. At the cutting edge of this lamentable popular genre, one finds Jacob Helberg's *The Wires of War* (2021). Sitting at the intersection of government and Big Tech, Helberg personally epitomizes much of what is laughable about the pushers of the fake China Threat. Really, one must fight the urge to laugh at the idea of a former Google and government "disinformation" commissar warning us of the perils to Americans' privacy due to the collusion of government and Big Tech.

To be sure, the Chinese government has great interest in collecting as much personal data as it can; but, of course, so, too, does the American government. And herein lies the problem; for while critics of such an equivocation will garrulously babble something about the Fourth Amendment and the ostensible accountability of democratically elected governments, no one who has been paying attention at all for the last twenty years can be confused as to how much the national security state cares about Americans' right to privacy. Between cries of "If you aren't doing anything wrong, why do you care?" and "Well, better the American government than the Chinese government," one can, from time to time, get a word in edgewise, pointing out that, by these government apologists' own admission, the federal government spies on millions of Americans annually and that the Kafkaesque nightmare of the FISA system means that virtually anyone could be unknowingly subject to total surveillance by the government at any time, for virtually any reason.

In short, the digital age has made the kind of snooping that once had to be conducted physically far too easy for any government to resist. They claim national security, and enough people buy it to make holding them accountable and getting them to stop virtually impossible. The individual can choose not to participate, not to use various products, and to minimize his digital footprint as much as possible, but beyond that, there is little someone actually concerned about the civil liberties of society generally can do; such liberties simply seem not to be valued by the greater majority. That being said, the recent efforts to ban TikTok, like the earlier campaign against Huawei, are not being conducted by disinterested public servants. Among the biggest spenders when it comes to lobbying are domestic technology and manufacturing firms, who would like nothing better than to keep foreign rivals out in order to protect their market power and their place as gatekeepers of what counts as truth.

Opportunity for yet more statist hackery has been furnished by Washington's sudden determined interest in cutting off Beijing's access to certain kinds of high-end microchips. Here, Chris Miller's *Chip War* (2022) takes the top billing. As yet another unashamed careerist hawker of the latest thing you should be afraid of, his résumé furnishing as much of an indictment to his credibility as Helberg's (the American Enterprise Institute, Hoover Institute, Transatlantic Academy, and Brookings Institute), Miller's contributions to the degradation of the public dialogue surrounding U.S.-China relations have been as significant as the pretended debates about what would happen were Beijing to capture those high-tech fabs in Taiwan are pointless. For one thing, Beijing has made no move to do anything of the kind and is heavily reliant on trade with Taiwan; for another, as former National Security Advisor Robert O'Brien has stated publicly, U.S. policy is to destroy those very factories should Beijing attempt to seize Taiwan.[48] The casual criminality of such an act aside, the idea that the United States should go to war with Beijing over Taiwan because of these semiconductors, a position openly espoused by Chairman of the House Foreign Affairs Committee Michael McCaul (R–TX), is as criminal as it is stupid.[49]

The choices of free-market actors aside, whatever the impact of lobbying (to be addressed momentarily), if Washington were so concerned about the fact that for years upwards of 90 percent of the world supply of these semiconductors was located on an island 80 miles from China and which is recognized by it and the international community as part of China,

---

[48] Steve Clemons, "The U.S. would destroy Taiwan's chip plants if China invades, says former Trump official," Semafor, March 13, 2023.

[49] From Representative Michael McCaul's April 8, 2023, interview, "'Best Deterrence' to Xi in Taiwan is Failure for Putin in Ukraine." Interviewed by Chuck Todd on *Meet the Press*.

efforts should have been made to address it long ago. Those efforts, as an aside, are now being taken — much to the concern, it should be noted, of Taiwan Semiconductor Manufacturing Company (TSMC) representatives, for both economic and geopolitical reasons. Given that semiconductors are often referred to as the "oil" of the digital economy, and that Washington's increasingly aggressive efforts to cut China off from them seem to mirror nothing so much as the FDR administration's blatant attempts to push the Imperial Japanese government into kinetic war by way of gradual economic war, Americans should read with alarm the glowing reports in the *Wall Street Journal* and elsewhere that Washington has successfully bullied the Dutch, Japanese, British, or Koreans into getting on board with the chip war against China.[50]

In conclusion, conflicts of interest abound when talking about China and the fake China Threat. But more important than the fact that outlets like Politico are literally being brought to you by Lockheed Martin, or that the "experts" appearing on CNN or FOX come from think tanks funded directly by D.C. or by foreign governments (like Taiwan's), is that it cannot be otherwise, given the reality of the American empire.[51] This is not to deny any of the actors involved their due agency, turning them into nameless automatons incapable of doing otherwise; these people do have names, and they could in theory do otherwise. What prevents them from doing so, what prevents anyone from doing so in their position, is that their actions become a function of their position within the structure of power in which they exist. After all, is it any surprise that Taiwanese politicians and manufacturers would sooner spend a few million dollars lobbying Washington and Silicon Valley than undertake the floating of supercarriers that cost orders of magnitude more? Or that starving, debt-laden graduate

---

[50] Desirous of war, but unwilling to be seen precipitating it, see then-Secretary of State Henry Stimson's remark "the question was how we should maneuver them [the Japanese] into the position of firing the first shot without allowing too much danger to ourselves," U.S. Congress, *Hearings Before the Joint Committee on the Investigation of the Pearl Harbor Attack* (Washington, 1946), page 5433. As a saving grace, China can at least make semiconductors, whereas 1930–40s Imperial Japan could not make oil or iron ore, and recent reports suggest China's domestic semiconductor production has increased dramatically in the last years.

[51] See the terrific work of Ben Freeman at the Quincy Institute for detailed analyses of the variety of (entirely legal) influence-buying operations taking place daily in Washington.

students will scramble over one another to write about the dangers facing America and the world should the empire yield a single inch? No, it isn't surprising. But what is surprising is that those standing outside the structure of power (i.e., most Americans) continually allow themselves to be so used in its service. Helping Americans to understand themselves as victims of the Empire little different from the helpless millions of innocent men, women, and children of Iraq, Syria, Libya, Afghanistan, and Yemen, killed or dispossessed under the flimsiest pretenses of either our own safety here or their own betterment there, is the job of loyal, unconflicted public intellectuals.

Chapter 9:
Uyghurs, Genocides, and Realities

In January 2021, as he was on his way out the door, outgoing Secretary of State Mike Pompeo dropped a diplomatic bombshell, accusing the Chinese government of genocide against its minority Uyghur population.

There is, frankly, a lot to unpack in this allegation. Before getting too much into the matter, let's start with just a few basics about the legal definition of *genocide* as a preliminary. This is important because most people, when they hear "genocide," imagine something like what happened in Rwanda in 1994, when somewhere north of half a million people were exterminated along ethnic lines. And while this is the popular understanding of "genocide," and large-scale killing along ethnic lines of course qualifies, Article Two of the Convention on the Prevention and Punishment of the Crime of Genocide defines *genocide* as "any of the following acts committed with the intent to destroy, in whole or in part, a national, ethnical, racial, or religious group."

The list is as follows:

1. Killing members of a group

2. Causing serious bodily or mental harm to members of the group.

3. Deliberately inflicting on the group conditions of life calculated to bring about its physical destruction in whole or in part.

4. Imposing measures intended to prevent births within the group.

5. Forcibly transferring children of the group to another group.

Clearly, then, the international legal standard for genocide is much broader than simply the targeted killing of the members of a group. Two points about the diction of the clause are worth noting before diving into the particulars of the case of the Uyghurs. First, "any" of the above acts constitutes genocide — but only, according to the clause, if committed with the "intent" to destroy, in whole or in part, the group in question.

So, what is a Uyghur, and was Mike Pompeo right?

First, the Uyghurs are a Turkic-speaking Muslim minority group primarily located in what is today Northwestern China. Ancient history aside, it was brought under Chinese control in the 1700s as part of the "Ten Great Campaigns" of the Qing dynasty, which saw the Chinese Empire reach its greatest territorial extent. Unlike Washington, whose policy was to dispossess totally and intern those ethnic minorities whose land they conquered in order to establish settler colonial populations, the Uyghur were largely left in place, and efforts to introduce a Han Chinese population were only minimally successful.[52]

While still permitted to practice their culture and religion, the Uyghurs had a long history of independence, and they chafed under military rule, with rebellions and revolts featuring prominently. As the Qing dynasty disintegrated and the factions of the fledging Republic of China fought among themselves (and against the Japanese), these efforts culminated in 1933 with the establishment of an "East Turkestan" as a breakaway Islamic Republic constituted of part of western Xinjiang. It lasted barely a year and was destroyed by forces allied with the Kuomintang (KMT). A second state of East Turkestan would be re-established in 1944 before this too was quickly snuffed out, this time by the triumphant CCP. Oddly enough, Mao and subsequent leadership in Beijing also chose to leave this ethnic minority group largely to itself, even excluding it from the harsh social engineering projects to which they subjected the rest of the population.[53]

This began to change over the decade of the 2010s, with the same standards of population control beginning to be applied to the Uyghurs. This coincided with a rise in terrorist attacks in Xinjiang and in other areas of China committed by members of the East Turkestan Islamic Movement.[54] With endemic poverty, high birthrates, and highly visible crime connected with the region, as well as its centrality to the Belt and Road Initiative, it was little wonder when Beijing began to focus its attention on Xinjiang.

According to Mike Pompeo and the U.S. State Department,[55] that increased attention by Beijing took the following forms: mass surveillance; restrictions on freedom of movement, speech, assembly, and worship; as well as "forced sterilizations and abortions on Uyghur women, [coercing] them to marry non-Uyghurs, and [separating] Uyghur children from their families."

---

[52] When the PLA reconquered the territory in 1949, it was estimated that fewer than 10 percent of the population were of ethnic Han Chinese descent.

[53] Here meaning the two-child, then the one-child policies draconianly enforced.

[54] 18 terror attacks in a decade in the region (from 2007–2016) — as well as an attack claimed by the primary group responsible (the East Turkestan Islamic Movement) on Beijing in 2013, as well as the massive Kunming attack of 2014.

[55] Mike Pompeo, "Determination of the Secretary of State on Atrocities in Xinjiang," January 19, 2021.

These are extremely serious accusations. The latter list strikes one as particularly heinous. If true, taken together, these would clearly, even in the absence of mass killing, meet the criteria for genocide. However, the evidence provided to back up these incendiary claims is virtually nonexistent, scant, or as problematic as the notion that Mike Pompeo is defending Muslims in China "because it is right" and not simply because it is a convenient stick with which to smack Beijing.

First, much of the documentation prominently features a German anthropologist of frankly questionable scholastic character and fitness.[56] Debates about methodology, reliability, bias, and conflicts of interest aside, however, people are being locked up on a large scale for things no classically liberal person could consider reasonable. Many of the activities for which there is evidence constitute major human rights violations. Fining, imprisoning, and surveilling the population of the province intensively for a combination of violating laws on the number of children one may have or on suspicion of terrorism is beyond heavy-handed. Equally certain, however, regarding the most serious accusations (those of mass sterilization, forced abortion, and coerced marriages) the evidence is either lacking or overstated.[57]

Second, despite the constant chorus of insinuations by the United States, some of its allied governments, and their compliant corporate media, China has been charged with nothing by the UN, and those governments who have cared to weigh in have sided almost two-to-one with Beijing.[58] Are Uyghurs being discriminated against? Maybe. Maybe

---

[56] See Gareth Porter and Max Blumenthal's extensive look into Zenz's work, entitled: "U.S. State Department Accusation of China 'Genocide' Relied on Data Abuse and Baseless Claims by Far-Right Ideologue," published at the *Grayzone*, February 18, 2021.

[57] Even the Associated Press, which has followed along with the rest of the Western corporate media in the chorus of "genocide," concede as much, noting: "Having too many children is a major reason people are sent to detention camps… with the parents of three or more ripped away from their families unless they can pay huge fines." Acknowledging Beijing is essentially extending its general (terrible) policies to the Uyghurs as evidence of Beijing "aggressively promoting intermarriage," they cite the testimony of "one couple" (see Works Cited).

[58] Initially 22–35, the latter number rose to 54, both groups writing open letters to the U.N. Human Rights Council, the former condemning and the latter defending (see Works Cited).

even probably. But should that serve as the basis of policy toward Beijing? Assuredly not. Such discrimination is hardly unique, nor is having an abysmal human rights record. This does not prevent the likes of Egypt or a host of other authoritarian states from sitting comfortably on the U.S.'s payroll. It is obvious to everyone, allies, frenemies, and foes alike, why Washington has decided to make the Uyghurs an issue: it serves their interests.

It doesn't serve the American people's interest, but then virtually none of Washington's chosen policies do.

Chapter 10:
Facing Unpleasant Facts, or Washington's Revanchism and Revisionism

With so much having been made in the past decade over China's behavior in its immediate neighborhood — from jousting with Japan over the Senkaku/Diaoyu Islands to building up and occupying the Spratly Islands, from harassing Filipino fishermen to engaging in actual border clashes with India — it is worth stepping back and taking a wider view of Chinese behavior in its immediate vicinity. Is it unprecedented? How did other large, rising, militarily capable states behave? How, for example, did the rising United States behave? Spoiler alert: compared to the rising colossus of the late 19th century United States, Beijing has displayed considerable restraint.

"Our Little Region Over Here"

Note that by beginning our examination in the late 19th century, from the outset we pass over the aggressive and violent expansion of the territorial bounds of the United States up to the dawn of the 20th century, when the size of the United States increased almost twelvefold. During that time, besides the American Revolution, War of 1812, Barbary Wars, and Mexican American War, the U.S. fought no fewer than four dozen wars against the various Amerindian tribes and confederations that had previously held sway over the vast bounds of the western North American continent. So, too, we pass over its involvement in East Asia, in the Opium Wars and Korea and Japan — which it forced open at gunpoint in 1853. But the plain fact is this: from its inception to the "closing of the frontier" in 1890, the U.S. was engaged in armed conflicts of one kind or another with its various neighbors for almost 80 percent of its existence.

But by 1890, the United States, officially having declared complete its self-appointed mission of manifest destiny, to spread itself from Atlantic to Pacific, quickly turned its gaze abroad. The transformation of the relationship of the states to the federal government during the Civil War, as well as rapid industrialization and the spread of telegraph and railroad lines, meant that the U.S. was increasingly capable of projecting concentrated force abroad. Its interactions with other major powers over the following decades illustrate plainly one of the foundational realist principles of international relations: as its relative power increased, so, too, did its demands for deference in its immediate vicinity. Indeed, as soon as it had achieved the requisite levels of internal cohesion and industrial might, it set about enforcing its hitherto nominal regional hegemony.

While the Monroe Doctrine was initially set forth in 1823, the principle that henceforth the Western Hemisphere was off limits to further meddling from outside powers was, to quote the political scientist Graham Allison, "largely aspirational rather than actual." It did not, for example, prevent Great Britain from treating South America as a de facto part of its Empire, seizing the Falklands from Argentina and routinely intervening in the domestic politics of places like Nicaragua and in the islands of the Caribbean. So, too, a decrepit Spain still held Cuba, a mere 90 miles from the U.S. mainland. And by the 1880s, following German unification, the German Imperial Navy became a regular and unwelcome presence in Latin America.

No more: henceforth, the Monroe Doctrine would be enforced and even the mightiest of the European great powers made to observe it. When the British threatened to intervene in Venezuela over unpaid debts and a disputed border, President Grover Cleveland's Secretary of State Richard Olney warned the British: "Today the United States is practically sovereign on this continent, and its fiat is law upon the subjects to which it defines its interposition."

That was in the mid-1890s. By 1902, on the heels of the decisive U.S. victory over Spain in Cuba and the Philippines, and with U.S. industrial and military power still rapidly expanding, the British and Americans once again found themselves on opposite sides of a border dispute — this time about the exact boundary between the U.S.'s Alaskan Territory and Western Canada. President Theodore Roosevelt made it known that: "In the event of specious and capacious objections on the part of the English, I am going to send a brigade of American regulars up to Skagway and take possession of the disputed territory and hold it by the power and the force of the United States."

In addition to helping make the Monroe Doctrine a reality, Roosevelt would add his own corollary: any state in the region unable to maintain its own internal order, or which displayed "impudence" to the U.S., might now be subject to military intervention. On his way to deploy U.S. troops to intervene in the domestic politics of a half-dozen Central American and Caribbean countries during his time in office, a policy that would be dutifully followed by all of his predecessors until his cousin took office in 1932, the Rough Rider President had this to say in response to those who criticized blatant U.S. violations of other states' sovereignty: "The Monroe Doctrine is not a question of law at all. It is a question of policy. To argue that it cannot be recognized as a principle of international law is a mere waste of breath."

He could as well have quoted the Roman general Pompey ("Don't quote laws to men with swords!") or the earlier Greek general Thucydides ("The strong do as they will and the weak suffer what they must").

Looking in the Mirror

The British displayed prudence in their decisions to de-escalate situations of transitional friction as its relative power declined, thereby avoiding costly and distant wars with a rising power it couldn't afford over peripheral issues.

U.S. actions, while a distant memory by the standards of our own brief historical life as a nation, appear in the eyes of the 2,000-year-old Chinese something like a fortnight ago. Thus does U.S. posturing today seem to them wildly hypocritical and nakedly self-serving: having gotten what we want, we want to call the game.

This is especially irritating when it comes to Taiwan/Taipei, a province which everyone, from the UN to the United States, acknowledges as part of China, and which but for the opaque, and now under President Joe Biden explicit, threat of U.S. military intervention would now be securely back under Beijing's control. That the island is strategically valuable is granted — so, too, that its democratic and technological achievements are laudable — but is a now eight-decade-old civil war supposed to continue indefinitely? As their positions of relative strength change, both in the region and elsewhere, militarily as well as economically and diplomatically, is China expected to put up with this state of affairs? How, one wonders, would the American public, media, political, policy, and military elite react if China were to sign a basing agreement with Brazil, or Russia with Venezuela?

As the only attempted probing of the Monroe Doctrine since Teddy Roosevelt's time resulted in the Cuban Missile Crisis, I think it's safe to say we know the answer.

Conclusion

George Orwell prided himself on being able to face unpleasant facts; that quality he believed most qualified him to be novelist and commentator. And in this case, the unpleasant fact is that the U.S. behaved no differently from how Beijing is now behaving when it was in Beijing's relative geostrategic position, and would behave no differently were the situation reversed. Indeed, from Reagan to Obama, it has been regular tradition for U.S. administrations to thumb their noses at both international court rulings and international opinion when they run contrary to their perceptions of America's interests — as in the cases of mining Nicaraguan harbors and Middle East drone bombing campaigns.

With public polls revealing increasing support among the American public for military intervention in defense of Taiwan's claim to territorial autonomy, the American public would do well to pause and reflect on how what China wants is recognition and control of, in the case of Taiwan, its internationally recognized borders. The American public should also not be misled into thinking that the question of Taiwan's status can be indefinitely put off through clever diplomacy or the threat of American military intervention. Already simulated military conflicts over the island have the U.S. side losing regularly.[59]

Especially since Beijing's crackdown on Hong Kong dispelled any illusion as to its ultimate fate, Taiwan's domestic politics have increasingly trended towards independence, and this is unlikely to change.[60] In truth, however, the minute Nixon set foot in Beijing, the matter was decided: if Beijing is the legitimate government of China, and Taiwan is part of China, ipso facto Taipei belongs to Beijing.

The U.S. has interfered in Chinese affairs for well over a century. It's time we said enough is enough. That is not isolationism; it is abandonment of an inconsistent, untenable, and indefensible foreign policy.[61]

---

[59] The Jan. 2023 war games by the Center for Strategic and International Studies projected U.S./Japan/Taiwan success in repelling a conventional amphibious assault, although the operation would cost: "dozens of ships, hundreds of aircraft, and tens of thousands of servicemembers" (see Works Cited).

[60] Of course, Taiwan's politics are not unidirectional and the KMT, as opposed to the Democratic Progressive Party, have generally upheld to a much more conservative, status quo line.

[61] With this section sure to have raised charges of "Whataboutism," it is worth noting that "Whataboutism" is simply a rhetorical device used by defenders of

the U.S. government's own crimes to enable them to act as though history started this morning.

Chapter 11:
Who Writes About the Fake China Threat, and Why

Over the past decade and a half, one has probably gotten used to books peddling the fake China Threat popping up as occasional best sellers. From Martin Jacques's *When China Rules the World* (2009) to Michael Pillsbury's *The Hundred-Year Marathon* (2015), one could simply shrug and move on. Talk in policy circles and in the commercial media was still largely of Beijing's integration into the "liberal world order" as a "responsible stakeholder," and of the gains in trade made, and still to be made, in exchange between the United States and China. The transformation of China from global partner to enemy number one seemed to happen, in Hemingway's words, gradually, then suddenly. Indeed, despite Trump's early bellicosity when it came to China, the corporate media and press didn't immediately play along with the fake China Threat narrative. Rather, most proclaimed the folly of his trade war and seemed to revel in reporting the losses it was inflicting on American farmers, whose exports to China had been interrupted as a result of retaliatory tariffs.

In the background the slow, ominous drip of the China Threat narrative continued, however, with Graham Allison's *Destined for War* (2017). Then suddenly, *Stealth War: How China Took Over While America's Elite Slept* (2019) by Robert Spalding, *Deceiving the Sky: Inside Communist China's Drive for Global Supremacy* (2019) by Bill Gertz, *Has China Won?* (2020) by Kishore Mahbubani, *The Long Game: China's Strategy to Displace American Order* (2021) by Rush Doshi, *The World According to China* (2021) by Elizabeth Economy, *War Without Rules: China's Playbook for Global Domination* (2022) by Robert Spalding, *No Limits; the Inside Story of China's War with the West* (2022) by Andrew Small, *Red Carpet: Hollywood, China, and the Global Battle for Cultural Supremacy* (2022) by Erich Schwartzel — it was as though even before COVID-19 hit in 2020, exacerbating already strained relations between the United States and China, the movement had been underway to translate for the public the policies pursued by multiple U.S. administrations to contain China. It suddenly became unusual to pick up one of the so-called "papers of record," the corporate media giants, the *Wall Street Journal*, *New York Times*, or *Washington Post*, without encountering something about China presented as ominous or threatening. Indeed, by the time Hal Brands and Michael Beckley's *Danger Zone: The Coming Conflict with China* (2022) hit bookshelves in August, entire opinion pages of the major papers sounded like talking points from the 2017 U.S. National Security Strategy, 2018 U.S. National Defense Strategy, or 2018 special report from the U.S. Trade Representative, all of which painted China as a direct threat to vital U.S. interests that needed to be vigorously countered and contained militarily, geopolitically, economically, ideologically, and technologically.

While many of the books mentioned above are written in the breathless, alarmed manner of their earliest forerunners, *The China Threat* (2000) by Bill Gertz, or Edward Timperlake and William C. Triplett's *Red Dragon Rising: Communist China's Military Threat to the United States* (1999), there have been some notable exceptions which sought and obtained some measure of balance even when they could not completely escape the fake China Threat paradigm. Kevin Rudd's *The Avoidable War* (2022) and James Fok's *Financial Cold War* (2021) both do a reasonable job presenting the facts and perspectives of both Washington and Beijing on key issues, and have as their aim de-escalating the growing crisis that is the present state and trajectory of U.S.-China relations.

Tellingly, outright dissenters, those who questioned any part of the ascendent China narrative, were few. George Magnus's *Red Flags: Why Xi's China Is in Jeopardy* (2018) and Thomas Orlik's *China: The Bubble That Never Pops* (2020) both deserve credit for seeing through to the true mess that is China's economy. Though their critiques of the fake China Threat narrative are incomplete, scarcely touching on the demographic, environmental, and geostrategic mountains confronting Beijing, China's economy being central to everything else, the one-party CCP dictatorship included, one could argue that an expansion of their critiques is all one needs to cast the entire prospect of a future "Chinese Century" into serious doubt.

And it is here that a point needs to be clearly parsed, for there is a significant difference between China ruling the world in the manner the United States has done for the past three decades, and Beijing enjoying preponderance in its immediate environs and proportional heft for its relative weight elsewhere around the globe where its interests are concerned. For while it is increasingly unlikely that China's economy will ever surpass that of the United States, either in total or per capita output, and unlikely, too, that it will ever have the military reach enjoyed by

Washington, Beijing has nevertheless grown relatively powerful enough that it can assert and more or less get what it wants in its immediate environs. Trivial, obvious, or realistic though that may seem to the objective observer, to Washington this fact constitutes the whole of the real China Threat: that is, the existence of an independent China (or Russia, for that matter) is a threat to Washington's accustomed ability to do more or less whatever it wants, wherever it wants. As Trump's first Secretary of State Rex Tillerson pointedly stated, China "threatened the U.S. Navy's Pacific domination."[62]

Regarding conflicts of interest, while they are almost never stated upfront, it is easy for anyone concerned to discover who pays the people writing the above books. Hardly the product of merely concerned citizens or honestly interested academics, almost invariably they are produced by people with a direct financial or career interest in great power conflict, specifically with China. To take just a few examples, Robert Spalding, a retired Air Force General, is a current Hudson Institute Fellow. Grant Newsham and Jonathan Ward, whose respective books *When China Attacks: A Warning to America* (2023) and *The Decisive Decade: American Grand Strategy for Triumph over China* (2023) were the most recent additions to the fake China Threat literature as this book was going through final draft edits, were and are similarly employed by the Center for Security Policy, Forum for Strategic Studies, and the Atlas Organization. Elizabeth Economy is on the Council on Foreign Relations as well as the payroll of the Hoover Institute, while Hal Brands and Michael Beckley get their blood money from the American Enterprise Institute. Rush Doshi is employed by the Brookings Institute as the director of the "China Strategy Initiative," Andrew Small by the German Marshall Fund, et cetera. Together, these institutions rake in millions in direct contributions from Lockheed, Northrop Grumman, Raytheon, Pratt & Whitney, Boeing, General Atomics and General Dynamics, as well as from the U.S. and allied governments.

Hardly surprising that the recent popular books about China that managed to be the most objective were those written by authors with either no direct relationship with any such institutions, like Thomas Orlik (a Bloomberg economist) or James Fok (a financial markets professional), or only the most limited, George Magnus. While no guarantee, it is

---

[62] Bob Woodward, *Rage* (New York: Simon & Schuster, 2020), pp. 10–11.

imminently more reasonable to look for information about threats or potential threats to American national security from those whose livelihoods do not directly depend on some threat (real or imagined) existing. It is among these that the present author is included.

Chapter 12:
Taiwan's 2023 Elections are no Independence Referendum

Talk the last few weeks in the corporate press about Taiwan is that the Democratic Progressive Party (DPP) has the coming January presidential election in the bag.

They are probably right.

The opposition parties, the Kuomintang (KMT) and smaller Taiwan People's Party (TPP), recently failed to coalesce behind a single candidate, so the DPP's William Lai is almost certain to win. A self-described "practical worker for Taiwan independence," Lai, the current vice president to the exiting Tsai Ing-wen, has chosen former envoy to the United States Hsiao Bi-khim as his running mate, completing the most pro-independence ticket yet in the government's history—with Bi-khim described as an "independence die-hard."

However, this is not to say, as the corporate press are sure to in the days and weeks following the election, that this was a clear vote in favor of the independence line by the ordinary residents of the de facto self-governing island.

The truth is that the overwhelming majority of Taiwanese simply want things to remain the way they are, with Taiwan maintaining its de facto independence and never saying another word about it. According to a 2021 report by the Global Taiwan Institute, the number supporting an outright declaration of independence are as few as 5% of the population.[63] Hence, in an effort to calm feelings of unease, Lai has recently taken to repeating a formula he and the DPP have increasingly assumed: "We mut abide by the truth—which is what I mean by pragmatism—which is Taiwan is already a sovereign, independent country called the Republic of China. It is not part of the People's Republic of China."

---

[63] Hsiao, Russell (2021). "Taiwanese Preference for Status Quo Remains Constant Even as Views Harden," Global Taiwan Brief, Vol. 6, Issue 15.

While this may be "pragmatic" in a day-to-day sense, as far as his or anyone else's conducting of the daily business on the island, it cannot be accepted by American policymakers. For American policymakers and commentators to begin parroting this line would be in direct contradiction to the foundational formula worked out during the Richard Nixon administration, promulgated by the First Sino-American Joint Communique: that there is but one China, that Taiwan is a part of it, and that its legitimate government is located in Beijing.

Given this, it is hardly surprising to find that Beijing is not Lai's biggest fan. After Lai's trip this past fall to the United States, which Beijing views as a violation of the terms of the Second Communique, the joint Sino-American statement the Jimmy Carter administration signed to finally normalize relations in 1979, China's foreign ministry issued a statement calling him a "troublemaker through and through," saying that "Lai stubbornly adheres to the separatist position of Taiwan independence." At the same time, Beijing also lodged what has become the rote formulation that accompanies such visits: that China opposes any form of visit by "Taiwan independence separatists" to the United States.

It's been the modus operandi of Washington and its loyal corporate press mouthpieces to write off complaints by powerful and concerned rival states. But as evidenced in Eastern Europe, this trivialization can have severe consequences.

These high-level diplomatic visits are frowned upon by Beijing, and by any neutral reading of the Communiques they are clearly against the spirit if not the direct letter of those foundational joint-statements. These visits are quickly becoming yet another domestic political football, and therefore, should strike even the most usually imperturbable as irresponsible in the extreme. Readers will recall former Speaker of the U.S. House Kevin McCarthy just this past year, in the fall of 2022, falling all over himself trying to show he was as tough as Nancy Pelosi after she visited Taiwan, an embroglio itself stemming in no small part from the growing influence of the Taiwan Lobby.[64]

---

[64] Freeman, Ben (2022). "How the Taiwan Lobby Helped Pave the Way for

Like increased weapons sales and American troops being placed on the island, these leader-level visits do not increase American security or prosperity. And when the new (old) DPP administration is sworn in next year in Taipei, both Lai and those in Washington would do well to ignore the most hawkish and foolish on either side, the only ones who want to disturb the status quo.

It has held so far, and there is every reason to believe it can continue to do so if level heads prevail.

Pelosi's Trip," *Responsible Statecraft*, the Quincy Institute.

Chapter 13:
Taiwanese Elections, TSMC, and Washington's Folly

With Taiwan's Presidential Elections now concluded, and the Democratic Progressive Party (DPP) candidate William Lai Ching-te having won a plurality due to the failure of the major opposition parties, the KMT and TPP, to combine behind one candidate, tensions in the region are likely to increase. As reported by Aljazeera, in the preceding weeks Beijing had (again) "denounced Lai as a dangerous separatist," and said he represented a "threat to peace in the region if he won." Neither surprising nor propitious, Lai being a staunch advocate of the island's independence, which he maintains is already de facto achieved, and Beijing having called the election a choice between "peace and war," as pressure on Taiwan by Beijing increases hawks in D.C. will doubtlessly trot out their favorite line in defense of furthering U.S. commitments to the defense of Taiwan: "But – we need those microchips!"

Setting aside the fact that official U.S. policy recognizes that there is one China, recognizes the official government to be that in Beijing, and acknowledges Beijing's claim that Taiwan is a part of China, thereby making the continued large scale sale of arms and the placement of U.S. troops on the island provocative to say the least, it representing continued intervention a seven decade long civil war – at least on the surface, dangling the threat of Taiwan's microchips being seized or destroyed seems something close to a winner for the hawks pitching the next round of conflict, certainly better than obviously empty rhetoric about democracy and human rights.

Beneath the surface, however, apart from the clear folly of provoking (another) conflict, one likely to be lost and anyway not able to be "won," whatever that means, at anything like an acceptable, realistic cost, the story of Taiwan semiconductor manufacturing and its centrality to the global economy is complicated, and its position in no way made safer by increased belligerence by Washington (or its clients) in the region.[65]

A bit of background on how we got here:

---

[65] Goldstein, Lyle (2017). "The US-China Naval Balance in the Asia-Pacific: An Overview," *The China Quarterly*, Cambridge University Press, Vol. 232.

First, as technology becomes more sophisticated it becomes more expensive to produce (obviously). In the case of a cutting edge "fab," that is a factory for manufacturing semiconductors or integrated circuits, these can cost upward of twelve billion dollars just to build. Back in the American manufacturing heyday, before the rise of globalized shipping and communication that made the highly diversified supply chains and on-demand ordering of today possible, companies such as Intel designed and manufactured chips in their own fabs. As rapid and cheap communications proliferated, by the mid-1980s companies such as AMD began to move away from this traditional, integrated mode of production: they began essentially contracting out the very expensive production of the actual product once its design had been perfected.

TSMC's founder, Morris Chang, took this basic possibility of borne of increasing globalization, to create a so-called "pure play" semiconductor fab: with the help of the Taiwanese government, which gave it one hundred million dollars in initial support, Chang created a company that would specialize *solely* in the manufacture of chips designed by others. By doing this it could focus its resources strictly on production and production improvements, which over time expanded into vast qualitative differences.

And while the search for cost savings initially drove firms like Qualcomm to look for strategic partners, what enabled TSMC to eventually grow into the only player in town was its commitment to being what the *Wall Street Journal* has called the "Switzerland of semiconductors." After all, one couldn't simply hand off the necessary sensitive information about their technological and business needs to rivals with spare fab capacity to produce what they needed (a previously common practice).

It was, therefore, this combination of cost savings, government assistance, commitment to privacy, fostering of strategic relationships, learning by doing, hub and knowledge economy effects, that over the course of decades made Taiwan into a critical node in the global economy. Though this happened relatively by accident, a breakaway province of China becoming so central to the burgeoning digital economy, timing is always a consideration, and it was precisely during the heady unipolar moment of the 1990s and early 2000s that TSMC really began to put distance between itself and its competitors. Who cares where things are located – it's the end of history and everything is going to wind up being effectively America's playground, right?

This, of course, was not to be.

Predictably, Washington's two-fold solution was to weaponize this critical chokepoint in the global economy, threatening to destroy the facilities itself in the event of a mainland invasion, and to start doling out absolutely massive corporate subsidies to rehome critical semiconductor manufacturing so as to insulate itself from the fallout of its hazardous geopolitical stratagems.[66]

Capitalizing on this fear, Intel's new CEO, Pat Gelsinger, predictably began milking the government for money – and this worked like a charm (though he complained when TSMC, a "foreign" company, was given similar subsidies to help build a factory in Arizona – since expanded to a second facility). For their part, TSMC had reportedly not wanted to go this route, but had "decided to move forward with the plant [in Arizona] because the U.S. government implored us to do it."[67]

As the *Financial Times* reported back in July, there are concerns inside the beltway that Lai, now the President of Taiwan, is a loose cannon, that his remarks in July regarding visiting the White House, for example, were "super unhelpful." Seeking to defuse that particular situation, the *FT* reported that despite claims by Taiwanese government spokespersons that Washington had subsequently been in contact and no longer had any "serious concerns" regarding the matter, the White House denied having made any such inquiries – highlighting why, according to Dennis Wilder, a former White House China official, why the Biden administration was "very anxious" about Lai.[68] Continuing, he explained to the *FT* that the Biden administration felt "hamstrung,' as "any public rebuke could spark [more] support for Taiwan from Congress." Indeed, the Taiwan lobby certainly makes sure the right pockets are being padded: "what," asked Wilder, "Can they [the Biden administration] actually use for leverage with a politician like Lai?"[69]

---

[66] McKinney and Harris (2021). "Broken Nest: Deterring China from Invading Taiwan," *US Army War College Quarterly: Parameters*, Vol. 51 No. 4.

[67] Farrell and Newman (2023). *Underground Empire: How America Weaponized the World Economy*, Henry Holt and Co: New York.

[68] Sevastopulo and Hille (2023). "Washinton presses Taiwan presidential frontrunner on White House Comments," *Financial Times*, July 19.

[69] Zhang and Freeman (2021). "The Taiwan Lobby," Center for International Policy, Foreign Influence and Transparency Initiative.

Indeed, what can the world empire do to reign in a client – maybe just commit to fighting a major war for them?

Combining the fear of moving too fast in provoking Beijing with the urgent push by Washington to gain cutting edge semi-conductor independence, the *Washington Post* mused that an "upset victory" by the KMT, the DPP's major opposition party, might be desirable as the election of the more Beijing friendly of Taiwan's political parties might buy Washington some quiet time to better prepare its "deterrent capabilities."[70]

Read: military buildup and attempted insulation of its own economy.

This is all folly.

Weaponizing interdependence will only prompt further decoupling, lowering the cost of a war between the United States and China. Given that such a war must not happen, the costs of going to war should be raised not lowered.

The status quo has worked out to everyone's advantage for decades; and only the most reckless or foolish would try to see it altered.

It was good to see, therefore, especially given some of his prior statements, that when Joe Biden was asked for a reaction to the elections, he stated: "We do not support independence."[71]

Hopefully he remembers that – and that the invariable rank opportunist hawks are ignored.

---

[70] Willick, Jason (2024). "Why a Taiwan election upset could be a U.S. blessing," *Washington Post*, January 5.

[71] Holland, Bose, and Hunnicutt (2024). "U.S. does not support Taiwan independence, Biden says," *Reuters*, January 13.

Conclusion

While China is far from a paper tiger, the real danger when it comes to U.S.-China relations isn't any direct threat Beijing poses to the United States or to the interests of the American people. Rather, the real danger is that an increasing belligerence emanating from Washington might provoke a disastrous conflict over what Beijing considers core Chinese interests. Particularly with its shift in posture over the past decade, from Obama's more geoeconomic approach to Trump's, and now Biden's, increasing militarization of relations between the two, Washington risks provoking a conflict over Taiwan, or in the South or East China Seas.

Knowing that there are certain red lines, as over Taiwan, that Beijing would have to respond to if crossed, it may be, as Robert Kagan argued this past year in *Foreign Affairs*, that U.S. policymakers think that they should push China into a confrontation now, when it is more likely to lose, than later, when they believe that Beijing's relative position will be even stronger. Such a loss would destroy the CCP's credibility, they argue, opening up the possibility of a change in political regimes at the same time it diminished China in the eyes of its neighbors and the world. This is a questionable assumption, however. While it would probably mean the end of Xi's time as leader, the institution of the CCP has weathered significant tumult before and could likely do so again. In fact, in the event of a conflict with the United States over one of its core interests, it is just as easy to imagine the opposite occurring. After all, the sense of a state under siege strengthens, rather than weakens, the hand of an authoritarian regime. In this sense, both the Trump and Biden administrations' actions and rhetoric are playing right into the CCP's grateful hands. Facing imminent multifront disasters, the now openly confrontational U.S.'s attitude is likely to give the CCP its best chance of staying in power as these crises all come to a collective head: by arguing that only it, the CCP, has been able to make China great again and prevent its exploitation by looming foreign imperialists, and that only it can protect China from a United States newly determined to subvert and dominate it.

Troublingly, though a conflict between the two could easily escalate to the point of a humanity-ending nuclear exchange, as well as the fact that China is unlikely ever to pose a serious threat to core American interests, there are many domestic forces here in the United States that are pressing just such an escalatory dynamic. From entrenched institutional interests within the military and security bureaucracies determined to hold on to their positions and power, to weapons manufacturers who want to see their contracts continually renewed or expanded, to think-tankers determined to avoid getting real jobs and a corporate media that has never seen a potential war it doesn't like, to a high-tech industry that would rather insource critical components from places like Taiwan in the name of saving a few bucks, as well as domestic manufacturing industries seeking insulation from Chinese competition, and Republicans and Democrats seeking to score cheap points by trading insults over who is "softer" on China: the situation is exceedingly dangerous. Though completely unnecessary, the "China Threat" being a clear canard, to paraphrase the late Justin Raimondo's "all foreign policy being domestic policy," none of the existing dynamics in play are likely to change — no matter how valid the criticism. And the American people, as well as the rest of the world, will have to just hold their breath and hope for the best.

Appendix:
Common Claims Debunked

While by no means comprehensive, the following is a short list of some odd claims one will commonly hear brought forward as a reason for confrontation or conflict with China.

1. *"China" owns TikTok.* Apart from the fact "China" doesn't "own" anything, ByteDance, the company that owns TikTok, is majority owned by investors outside of China. Beyond that, there has never been anything but speculation and innuendo regarding the amount of data shared by the company with the Chinese government.

2. *China is buying up all the U.S. farmland.* Again, it isn't "China" per se but rather Chinese individuals and companies, and the reality is that total Chinese farm holdings in the United States amount to less than 1 percent. Having none of their own, it makes sense. Further, as one of the best asset classes to have invested in over the past several decades, it also makes sense.

3. *China used lead in American toys to make American children less intelligent...* Yep, spend enough time talking to people on the Internet, and you actually will hear this. So, too, that China is going to use the UN, WHO, et cetera, to take over America.

4. *China hooked the U.S. on fentanyl.* Much like critics who claim that China stole all the manufacturing jobs, the effects of D.C.'s own policies are blamed on China, attributing a level of sagacity and capability totally unwarranted to a regime so incompetent that it once accidentally starved millions of its own people to death in pursuit of a backyard smelting initiative.

5. *China stole all the technology.* Again, supernatural ability is accorded to Beijing and Chinese companies where really any finger-pointing, if there is any cause for any, is at the American government and American companies. Apart from the fact that the overwhelming majority of technology acquisitions were done so perfectly legally via so-called "forced technology transfers," wherein American companies chasing the China market made bad deals, deals the American government signed off on wherever and whenever necessary. Further, the huge headline numbers purporting to show the impact of China's actual technology theft through corporate espionage (which is real) makes use of dubious methodological

means and are clearly meant to provoke outrage rather than reasoned debate.

A Broader History of Sino-American Relations

The following lecture was delivered at Spring Arbor University, October 2023, on the occasion of the annual Community of Learners

There is hardly anything more important to the future of the world than Sino-American relations. And that's quite a thing to say when looking at the state of the world these days. But over the long-haul these, the two largest economies, militaries, and navies on earth must find some way to coexist, or else there is going to be trouble for everyone. The aim of this talk is to outline the course of Sino-American relations. Because of the scope and importance of the task before me, then, I'm just going to dive right in, as there is a lot to cover and only 45 minutes because I want to save time at the end for questions. At the outset, suffice it say I was once an undergraduate here in English and Political Science. As you can see on that slide, I work for the Libertarian Institute, and I write books and articles about foreign policy, history, politics, and economics.

As I presume most everyone here is generally familiar with the history of the United States, my talk will follow Chinese history and I will be introducing the relevant intersections between the U.S. and China as we go along. The United States being less than three hundred years old, and the first recorded ruling dynasties of China dating back to the second millennia BCE, I will be beginning my narrative of Chinese history rather abruptly, and quite late. Fascinating though its antecedents are, considerations of the time allotted to us today demand that we start with the last of the several foreign dynasties that ruled the area we associate today with the Chinese state. This was the ethnically Manchu Qing Dynasty (1644-1911). These were the descendants of an earlier northern "barbarian," that is non-Han Chinese, people who had conquered northeast China in the early twelfth century, establishing the Jin Dynasty (1115-1234), which was subsequently destroyed by the Mongol Yuan Dynasty a hundred odd years later (1271-1368).

Like their conquering predecessors, the Manchus had been effectively Sinicized. That is, in a manner not dissimilar to the case of the Normans of Europe during the Middle Ages, the ruling Manchus merged with and in

71

important ways adopted Han Chinese culture, Confucianism, Taoism and Legalism. There were pragmatic reasons for this, and the reasons are in some ways central to the story of China in the 19th century, when it had its first sustained conflict with the newly industrialized states of Western Europe and the United States. You see, China is very large, the terrain is very challenging, and then as now it was extraordinarily populous. The Confucian bureaucratic elites and the existing governing structures were critical to anyone who wanted to effectively govern China, and prevent it from disintegrating into warring states, which happened at several points during Chinese history, most recently in the early 20th century.

Marshalling the considerable resources of the Chinese state, scholars estimate that at the time China accounted for fully forty percent of global output, the Qing thereafter brought the Chinese Empire to its greatest territorial extent, adding new territories in central Asia, such as the province of Xinjiang and in the adjoining seas, such as Formosa, that is Taiwan. The centrifugal forces that would fatally weaken, undermine, and ultimately destroy the Qing dynasty were already at work, however, and these are what you see up on the screen here.

Obviously, any one of these problems is going to pose a severe challenge to any regime. Population growth strained the capacity of China's non-industrialized agricultural sector at the same time a series of severe weather events put additional stresses on the ability of Chinese society to feed itself. Economically, local elites dominated markets that were in theory unified internally and without barriers. However, these markets were relatively limited by the vast distances involved and by the low level of urbanization and industrialization that had occurred. With regards to corruption, the problem was two-fold: on the one hand you had local elites who were resistant to obeying the central government, who were willing, for example, to let the British and Americans run opium into China in exchange for a cut of the action; while on the other hand, you have the more basic kinds of corruption like preferential treatment, bribery, et cetera. As for foreign interventions and rebellions, we'll have plenty to say about those on the next slide.

Though internally there was relatively free movement of goods, as well as networks of finance, outwardly it was protectionist and, by the standards of the time, heavily bureaucratized. This hadn't really mattered because for centuries there had been little the few visiting Europeans had to offer that the Chinese wanted, or that the Chinese government had wanted them to have. That last is, of course, is a reference to opium. Because there was one thing the primarily British, but also American, sailors were increasingly bringing that millions of Chinese increasingly wanted and that was opium. Poppies were being run from India and later the Ottoman empire, processed into opium on a couple of offshore locations, and then smuggled into the country. This was as lucrative for the British East India Company and other traders as it was destructive to Chinese society, and so the British government was loath to put a stop to the flow when asked by the Qing. When diplomacy failed to stop the incoming opium, the Qing administration under the Emperor Daoguang took steps to try and block off and interrupt the illicit trade – going so far as to destroy British owned stocks of opium in Canton, at that time the only trading outpost open to the Europeans. A little pressure by the East India Company in London, and with that the First Opium War had begun.

Like the Second Opium War, which as you can see was fought just over a decade after the conclusion of the First, and was primarily concerned with enforcing the terms of the treaty of Nanjing, the military operations of the western powers concerned were primarily naval. That is, they primarily involved the blockading and shelling of ports. As for their aims, the wars were concerned with the expansion of the Europeans, and Americans', privileges in China: these were things like extraterritoriality, the rights of citizens of, say, Great Britain, to not be subjected to Chinese authorities but rather to locally based British ones. The cession of so-called Treaty Ports, additional enclaves for foreign traders to do business, Shanghai perhaps being the most significant. And, lastly, the rights of Christian missionaries operating in China were protected. I'll have more to say on Christianity in China later.

So as we can see from the conditions imposed on the Qing by the Europeans in the various treaties we see listed on the slide, neither the Opium Wars, nor any of the subsequent interventions we're going to talk about by the European powers or the United States in China, had as their goal replacing the existing Chinese imperial system. In fact, several of the most important interventions in China by the other powers were operations conducted in order to protect the Qing from domestic opponents to its regime. Why did they do this? Well, essentially for the same reason conquering invaders like the Manchu or Mongols had allowed themselves to be incorporated into existing structures. The Europeans couldn't possibly have occupied China, and after the experience of India few, particularly in England, at this point by far the strongest power, wanted to try. Leading intellectuals and politicians, people like William Cobden, believed colonizing India had been a mistake, and they wanted the British presence in China to be all the benefits of commerce with none of the expense and baggage of direct rule. However, as one might expect, the increasing presence and domination of China by foreigners led to backlash against the Qing regime the Imperial powers were seeking to prop up. One of the many ironies of empire we see repeated over and over throughout history.

Now I want to emphasize that even prior to the arrival of the Europeans in force, the Qing had already faced at least two serious rebellions. Remember, these were outsiders who weren't entirely beloved by the Han, especially for things like the way they were forced to wear their hair, that is the shaved front of the scalp with the long braid. But the destabilizing effects of losing multiple wars helped spark a virtual rolling tide of rebellions during the second half of the 19th century. The most important of these were the Taiping (1850-64) and Boxer (1899-1901) Rebellions, both of which required varying amounts of Western intervention to put down in order the keep the Qing empire in place. Now, unfortunately we don't have time to go into these in any depth, but since we were just speaking about the ironies of empire – in the first case you have the Europeans helping suppress a native Christian uprising; while in the second, the Manchu Qing are quietly encouraging what are essentially Han Chinese Nationalists to rise up against their regime in an effort to in that way somehow throw off the European powers.

The events surrounding the Opium Wars kick off what is referred to by the Chinese as their "century of humiliation." Now, some of what we see up on the slide takes us beyond the narrative we've already covered, things like the Second-Sino Japanese War or the Betrayal at Versailles. And we will talk about both of those things; but I just wanted you to be able to see whole litany of events that constitute China's "century of humiliation" listed all together, to get a sense of the blow after blow China took. Really, it is somewhat remarkable China survived more or less in one piece, as we'll see. And the "century of humiliation" at the hands of the Western powers and the Japanese remains very relevant in Chinese propaganda today.

So as we talk more about China's "century of humiliation," one thing that needs understanding is that the Qing Imperial Court essentially invited in the Russians and Germans and the French to compete with the Americans and English in order to try and play the powers off one another, trusting that they couldn't agree on how to divide up China among themselves, hoping they would fight each other over it and that eventually these foreign barbarians would leave. You have to think, Chinese history is very long: I mean, the Han dynasty was founded in the 200s BCE. Barbarians come and go, the thinking went. But, unfortunately for the Qing strategists at the Imperial court, this was not what happened. Because by granting most favored nation status on each of the powers, each successive privilege negotiated away would then be demanded by all the rest of the powers. Meanwhile, Russia, France, Japan, and Germany all took turns picking away pieces of China – all of Manchuria in the case of Russia, the tributary kingdoms of Vietnam and Korea respectively in the cases of the French and Japanese, while even the lately formed German empire got in on the action seizing a port for itself in the 1890s. And when we look at the pair of maps on the slide, which hopefully you can all see ok, illustrate precisely what we've just been talking about. Now, it isn't just that opium, Christian missionaries, and foreign traders are flooding in, as had been the case from the 1830s-1850s, now China is losing its influence in key areas, even losing vast stretches of territory. In the case of places like Macau and Hong Kong, they wouldn't be returned to Chinese sovereignty until the 1990s.

America officially protested. However, it demanded an Open Door, when it came to China: that is to say no American could be denied the same treatment of any citizen, missionary, or trader of one of the conquering European powers. Washington also sent forces to fight on the side of the Europeans in the Second Opium War, seeing action at the battles of the Taku and Island Forts. It also sent punitive expeditions to Formosa, Taiwan, in 1867 and to Korea in 1871. And while these weren't directly leveled against Chinese people, that is they were directly fighting the native Paiwan and Koreans respectively, these were both areas extremely sensitive to China, a technical province in the case of Taiwan and one of its long-time tributary kingdoms in the case of Korea. On top of all this were things happening in the United States itself which served to further alienate Chinese opinion. These included what came to be regular incidents of anti-Chinese violence in the United States beginning in the 1860s and '70s, which culminated in the Chinese Exclusionary Act of 1882. It was renewed in 1892 and made permanent in 1902. It remained in place until 1943, and as you can imagine it is the type of policy that makes you unpopular to the people in question. In fact, after it was made permanent a boycott movement erupted in China in 1905, coinciding with well-documented outbreaks of violence and discrimination against the Chinese in the United States, most prominently in San Francisco and Boston.

With the Qing government effectively unable to stand up for its citizens rights at home or abroad, and being challenged internally by a resistant commercial class, increasingly empowered military governors, and secret underground republican movements, it is hardly surprising to find the last Imperial dynasty finally being consumed by revolution in 1911. For any interested vexillologists, I have up on the slide the banner of the Qing dynasty and both flags of the Republic of China, the short lived multicolored iteration as well as the more famous blue and red one still used by the Taiwanese today. Now, the fledgling Chinese Republic that emerged, however, still faced many of the same problems as that of the Qing. China was an under-developed, multi-ethnic stew; it was surrounded by enemies, and several potentially rebellious Chinese generals were also in the mix. Almost immediately, then, the new government is challenged by Imperial Japan. As we saw on the last slide, Tokyo laid down a series of humiliating demands that the Chinese republican government had to accept or else face the prospect of a totally hopeless war. It wasn't long and those Chinese generals we just mentioned did in fact revolt against the central government, each becoming in effect the rulers of their own little competing kingdoms: so began the so-called "Warlord Era."

Now, in the intervening years the Republican government, first under Sun Yat-sen and then under his successors, were trying to do all they could to get western assistance, and specifically American assistance. Because you see despite America being far from innocent, Washington had always officially objected to what the other European powers were doing in China; and, further, Washington had recently returned its share of the large indemnity the imperial powers had extracted from the Qing court following the suppression of the Boxer uprising of 1900. So while the United States was maybe considered only the best of a bad lot, it was still considered the best. And when Woodrow Wilson came onto the world scene talking about the rights of all peoples to self-determination, America briefly became something of a darling in China. A quick succession of Chinese Republican leaders agree to send many thousands of Chinese laborers to Europe to help man the factories and do other manual work in order to assist the allied powers in defeating Germany in World War One. Critically, however, this was done on the understanding that in exchange for this service the pieces of China occupied by the German Empire, such as Kiatschou Bay, would be returned to China. On top of this, the Chinese negotiators believed that a number of other arrangements the Chinese didn't like would be on the table for discussion as well, things like China regaining the right to collect its own taxes on the trade going in and out of the country, which it had lost decades prior to the Europeans.

Instead, none of this happened. You see, Woodrow Wilson didn't want to upset the Japanese because he feared they then wouldn't join his new League of Nations. And so rather than pressuring the Japanese to vacate the German holdings in China Tokyo had occupied in its minor contribution to the allied war effort, Wilson gave those parts of China to Japan. Now remember this is just a few years after those demeaning demands Japan had made, and those just a couple decades after the Sino-Japanese War that had effectively cost China Korea and Taiwan. So this was extremely unpopular. In fact many draw a straight line from this betrayal, as well as the simultaneous Soviet Union renunciation of all of Imperial Russia's former privileges in China, to the May 4th movement and the rise of communism in China. While this almost certainly overstates things, if however slightly, it did not help that at this time Washington under the Warren G. Harding administration elected to recognize a series of those warlords we talked about previously, who in a series of battles were taking turns occupying Beijing. This caused the Chinese Republicans to turn to the U.S.S.R. for support.

Very quickly, I just want to introduce a few key figures. Together these three men played a significant role in determining the outcomes we see today, both on the mainland and on Taiwan. On the left is Sun Yat-sen, a doctor, philosopher, and republican. He is central figure in the underground revolutionary movements in China, however he spends much of his time abroad, essentially in exile. This included time spent in the United States; in fact, he was in the United States, on a train passing through Colorado, when he heard the news in 1911 that the Qing dynasty had fallen. He returns to China and does briefly assume the role of president. However, despite his prestige Sun has no military or economic power, nor any broad constituency or apparatus for executing his vision for China and this led to his ultimately passing power to a military authority; for, as we talked about on the last slide, China was in real danger of completely coming apart. During his time out of power Sun forms the Guomindang or Kuomintang or KMT, the political party that today shares in the rule of Taiwan, and which under the leadership of the next man we're going to talk about, would be the ruling party of the Chinese Republic. Before moving on to talking about Chang Kai-shek, however, we should note that it was Sun Yat-sen who initially brokered an agreement between the KMT and the newly emergent Chinese Communist Party (CCP) to work together to defeat the half-dozen military juntas ruling different parts of China. This is part of a broader effort Sun during the last years of his life to bring together the disparate factions in China and thereby to unify the country.

After Sun died in 1925, leadership of the KMT eventually passed to the second man on our slide, Chang Kai-shek; Chang was one of Sun's lieutenants; in fact, when Sun was denied aid by the American government in the 1920s and a mission was sent to the Soviet Union to seek assistance it was Chang who led the delegation to Moscow. While Chang succeeded in securing military and economic assistance from Moscow, Chang neither liked nor trusted the CCP with whom he was now working to defeat the warlords. And after having unified a significant portion of the country, particularly in the south and east, in 1927 Chang turns on the CCP in a violent purge. We'll go into that more on the next slide in the broader context of the essentially two decade long civil war fought for control over China. But for now, suffice it to say that but for one brief respite, Chang and the KMT would be in conflict with the CCP until finally driven off the mainland in 1949. Now, even though Chang had effectively cemented his and the KMT's control over China the challenges they faced were enormous. And what efforts the KMT made to try and stabilize and develop the country were constantly being foiled – most principally by the Japanese Empire, which would invade a few years later, in 1931 and then in full-force in 1937, the beginning of the Second Sino-Japanese War we'll be talking more about. But, again, for now let's just note that when the KMT and CCP resume fighting following the defeat of Japan in 1945, the KMT are forced to retreat all the way to Formosa, which from here on out I'll simply being referring to as Taiwan. The island, eighty miles off the coast of China, was then ruled by Chiang and the KMT as a military dictatorship under effective U.S. protection. To the end of his life, in the early 1970s, Chiang insisted that his was the legitimate government of China. And up until at least the mid-1960s there are records of his asking for and consideration in Washington having been given, for help waging a campaign in order to dislodge the communists in Beijing.

Which brings us to the last man on our slide, no pun intended for any of you Marxists out there, Mao Zedong. He was a student during the revolution; a huge reader, he spent a lot of time during the late 1910s drinking in the classical texts of western liberalism and experimenting with different ideas. By the early 1920s he has experience in secret underground societies and the rudiments of revolutionary activities, organizing, et cetera; and it is at this point that he has fallen in with the Chinese communists. He was a central early member of the Chinese Communist Party, heading one of the branches. He had some peculiar ideas, such as the revolutionary potential of the peasantry, which orthodox Marxists found ridiculous. He also embraced collaboration with the bourgeois revolutionary forces represented by the KMT, at least whenever they were willing to collaborate with him. In fact he even holds positions in the KMT in the mid-1920s before Chiang's purge. Unlike many of his early, and frankly, rival comrades, like Li Lisan, one of Mao's primary focuses was on maintaining an independent armed force. And it is this core of several thousand men and women that formed the future People's Liberation Army (PLA). Mao was deeply nationalist, but at the same time he was totally averse to anything he judged backward, or which made China weaker, even when those things were aspects of Chinese cultural itself. This is one of the interesting differences one sees today in Chinese state propaganda, is its emphasis on China's thousands of years of history and its traditions: Mao waged aggressive cultural wars against traditionalism, as he saw it. To him, it was all part of teaching China and the Chinese to "Stand up," as he put it, after a century of humiliations at the hands of the western powers and Japan. Mao successfully navigates both Chiang and the Japanese, and he emerges at the end of World War Two clearly the strongest force in China. Americans present as part of the 1944 Dixie Mission to China attest to that. He's being helped by the Soviets, and will continue to be assisted by the

Soviets all the way through the 1950s, even after Stalin's death. Mao attempts to radically transform Chinese Society by way of a series of Five Year Plans, and he initiates the so-called "great leap forward," a series of forced agricultural and economic measures that result in millions of Chinese starving to death. In response to criticism by more conservative party members like Deng Xiaoping, Mao launches the cultural revolution in order to effectively decapitate opposition to his continued rule. His deteriorating situation domestically, as well as his increasingly fraught relations with Moscow and the Vietnamese, result in Mao approving of an attempt to reach out to Washington. He dies in 1976: just four years after Nixon's visit and three years prior to the normalization of relations between Washington and Beijing, which we'll talk about here shortly.

Okay, so with that background in mind, on the first column of the next slide we have the Warlords era, which we talked about – the dividing up of the new Chinese Republic during the late 1910s and 20s by what were effectively feuding military dictatorships. In response you have the United Front and Northern Expedition, this was the unification of the KMT and CCP; who, with the help of Soviet arms and money, begin effectively retaking control of the country. That being practically accomplished, that first column concludes with the betrayal and murder of many of the communists in 1927-28, the so-called "Canton Coup" and Shanghai Massacre. In the second column, 1928-45, we see reunification of most of China under the KMT; the CCP responded by launching a guerilla campaign, which resulted in their being forced to retreat, the so-called "long March" – that was in 1934. And just a few years later, 1937, bottom of the second column, the Second Sino-Japanese War begins. And this horrifying eight year war quietly humming along in the background of world war two resulted in the deaths of somewhere close to 20 million people.

Now, this third column, I want to just pick up the story with the onset of the Second-Sino Japanese War and World War Two because the United States, though it sympathized with China and viewed Japan as a threat, it didn't want to fight Japan on China's behalf. And, indeed, though it would eventually in the late 1930s and early 1940s, begin sending aid and advisors to China, Washington's support was far from whole-hearted. It was a distant third priority behind Europe and the island hopping campaign in the Pacific. Washington did send missions, like the Dixie and Marshall missions, but their reports of the situation were largely negative. Marhsall, who is there after the end of the war against Japan tries to push for the creation of a unity government of the KMT and CCP. This of course failed and the Civil War resumed. But when it did it was quickly won by the communists. There are a number of reasons for this, the principle two being that Chiang's government was unpopular, ineffective, and corrupt, and the CCP had been receiving a steady supply of arms and funds from the Soviet Union. Mao and his forces sweep south, and the Americans watch as Chiang gets all of his army that he can across the strait to the islands of Taiwan.

And now, before we move on to the fourth column, which as you can see is headed by the Korean War, which I expect most of you already know a good deal about, I want to introduce you to something far less well-known and which isn't on the slide. This is the so-called China White Paper issued by the U.S. State Department in 1949, the year of the CCP's victory of the KMT on the Chinese mainland. In it, Secretary of State Dean Acheson and his team outlined why they felt that despite U.S. help the KMT was always going to fall to the CCP for the reasons already outlined, and why in their opinion a communist victory was not necessarily bad for U.S. interests. In fact, Acheson very perceptibly argued that the new regime in Beijing would be effectively nationalist and much like the Yugoslav Communist ruler Josep Broz Tito prove to be a thorn in the side of the U.S.S.R. rather than some plaint proxy. Korea changes that, however. With Stalin's encouragement the Korean communists controlling the northern half of the Peninsula attacked the south in response to shelling and sorties against them by the south which had been taking place in the several months prior. The U.S. intervenes, just keeping the communists out of Seoul; it drives them back across the dividing 39th parallel and the general in charge, MacArthur orders the forces under his command to pursue and drive them to the Yalu River – the border between Korea and China despite intelligence coming in that hundreds of thousands of Chinese troops sent by Mao were preparing to come pouring across to fight them. Of course, they do; they push the Americans back, my grandfather among them; and after a bloody couple of years, millions dead, the war essentially ends back where it started – and of course the situation of an armed truce continuing to this day.

Now, some historians argue that the entire debacle in Korea resulted from Acheson omitting Korea from a list of protected U.S. allies in east Asia during a public address he made. And while it is unclear precisely how much that played into the decision, it seems likely that it was a factor – and so in order to deter any other potential misunderstandings both Truman and then Eisenhauer make big shows of force across the Taiwan strait to deter what appears to be a looming threat by the CCP to invade across the 80 or so miles of water separating Taiwan from the mainland to finish off the KMT holed up on Taiwan. This results in a pair of war scares, in 1954 and then again in 1958, the first and second Taiwan Strait Crises, which see Eisenhauer openly threaten to nuclear bomb China. Eisenhauer did this a lot – in Korea, later in Indochina, that is Vietnam when it became clear the French were losing their battle against Ho Chi Minh and the Vietnamese Communists who would later go on to defeat the Americans as well. But importantly for Taiwan, the events surrounding the crises, particularly the Cold War and McCarthyism in the United States, resulted in Washington granting Taipei military protection via a mutual defense treaty in 1954.

Now I know you're all getting tired of this slide, but we're almost done and I'm going to move through the years faster on these last few – beginning with the Sino-Soviet split. Following the death of Stalin, in 1956 his successor Nikita Khruschev gives a quite incredible speech to a gathering of communist elites. Named "on the cult of personality and its consequences," Khruschev essentially denounces Stalin for being a murderous and repressive dictator. Now Mao does not like this. After all, he is well on his way to being the personality around which a cult is being formed. Furthermore, he actually liked and respected Stalin despite what he recognized to be Stalin's frequently duplicitous dealings with the CCP over the years. And so Mao denounces Khruschev, and by the early 1960s China is competing for influence with Moscow in the developing world. This was as Acheson had predicted, and indeed there are internal documents from the 1960s that speculate on the possibility of the U.S. allying with China, but it isn't until the election of Richard Nixon that any attempt to act on these insights are made. Now the background to this is that Nixon wants out of Vietnam, and he thinks the CCP can help exert leverage on the North Vietnamese; he also believes, correctly as it turns out, that this new front of the Cold War would push the Soviet's, now under the leadership of Brezhnev, towards strategic arms negotiations. And so Nixon sends his

National Security Advisory Henry Kissinger secretly to China via Pakistan to lay the groundwork for the normalization of U.S.-China relations. This ultimately resulted in Nixon's surprise trip to Beijing in 1972 and the production of a joint document known as the Shanghai Communique. This was the first of the three communiques you see at the bottom of that last column. The second, under the Carter administration in 1979, resulted in the official recognition of the government in Beijing. And the third we'll talk about on the next slide.

Before getting to that Third Communique, and further explaining the context and consequences of the normalization of relations between the U.S. and China, specifically for Taiwan, I want to quickly summarize what we've just gone over.

Following the fall of the final Chinese Imperial Dynasty, the Qing, from 1911-49 we have general if often limited support for the Republic of China from Washington. From 1949-72, we saw adversarial relations between Washington and the new People's Republic of China. 1972-82 brought rapprochement with the People's Republic of China to isolate the Soviet Union. And then, as we'll see here in a minute, from 1982-1991 under Deng Xiaoping the People's Republic of China pursues increasing privatization and integration into the global economy while maintaining good relations with Washington.

So, with the Second Communique Taiwan's relationship with the United States is officially altered. Now all three of the communiques are primarily concerned with Washington's respect for Chinese sovereignty, but the first communique is limited to establishing that "both sides acknowledge there is but one China and that Taiwan is part of it." It is with the Second Communique, in 1979, that the mutual defense treaty with Taiwan is ripped up and replaced with the Taiwan Relations Act as Washington now officially acknowledges Beijing to be home to the official government of China. Now not everyone is happy about this change, first and foremost Taipei, that is the KMT government on Taiwan. And they have friends and supporters in Washington, and they push back on the perceived weakening of U.S. commitments to the island with the Six Assurances; these follow the Third Communique under the Reagan administration, 1982, which had been almost entirely about Taiwan, and they are meant to reassure Taipei that the United States isn't about to stop providing them the means to defend themselves. Now, as Beijing agreed to work toward peaceful reunification but refused to rule out the possibility of retaking the island by force, Washington decided to maintain a posture of what's called "strategic ambiguity," that is there is no longer a guarantee to Taiwan that a mainland invasion will be met by U.S. forces, but nor is it ruled out: the idea here was to keep both sides guessing, and in that way prevent either Beijing from attempting to invade or Taipei from declaring independence, since that is basically Beijing's one red line that they say will trigger an automatic invasion of the island.

But under Deng in the 1980s Beijing has other things on its mind. It has received most favored nation status from the United States and is in the process of beginning to transform China. I want to emphasize that changes undergone in China over the past forty years have virtually no parallel, from how weak and unstable it was politically, economically, and militarily to where it is now. The best comparison is probably the newly unified German empire from 1870 to the onset of World War One. It did wage one war, but it was one the U.S. supported, that against the Vietnamese, who had removed the Pol-Pot regime from power in neighboring Cambodia. It also assisted Washington in Operation Cyclone, the arming of the Mujahadeen to bleed the Soviets in neighboring Afghanistan. So, all in all things seem to be proceeding well.

Then come the 1990s. Obviously, the end of the Cold War and then the collapse of the Soviet Union drastically changed Beijing's strategic calculations. They had fought multiple wars against the Soviets and the Russians before them; the two share a long border, and much of Beijing's war planning and resource allocation had thus gone toward bolstering their ground forces. On top of that change in its perceived threat environment to the north, Washington was taking its first steps as a unipolar power, and with virtually every move Washington made it alarmed or alienated the Chinese. First was Iraq War One, Desert Storm, which demonstrated that the United States' military was vastly superior to anything else in existence. Washington then immediately turned its defensive alliance, NATO, into an offensive alliance by intervening multiple times in the Balkans. And even more than the fact that this was Russia's backyard, was that the U.S. went in without a U.N. resolution authorizing the use of force, and then mistakenly bombed the Chinese embassy in Belgrade. So not good. The Clinton administration also threatened China over Taiwan. This was the so-called "Third Taiwan Strait Crisis," in 1996. What had happened here was that Taiwan was in the process of democratizing, and in fact the first Presidential Elections were about to be held, and Taiwan's President Lee was petitioning to visit his alma mater, Cornell. When he is let into the United States and gives this speech at Cornell, Beijing responds by firing missiles into the waters surrounding Taiwan. Now Beijing probably was overreacting – and certainly it was counterproductive, helping sour voters on Beijing's preferred candidates – however the Clinton administration's reaction was equally shocking: he called out the fleet and sent aircraft career battle groups to the Taiwan Strait. This was the same thing that had happened during the 1950s, when Eisenhauer had forced Beijing to back down with the threat of war.

Now despite these geopolitical problems in the relationship, at the beginning of the 21st century Sino-American relations were largely considered in an okay state due to the economic relationship developing between the two. Now this is happening on multiple levels: on one level you have U.S. corporations enjoying huge cost savings by relocating factories to China; they and their shareholders love that. Then you have U.S. consumers paying lower prices and getting lower interest rates on loans because the gains from globalization allowed for a loser central bank monetary policy. Then there were development theory and democratic peace theory, which together said that economic development brought democratization and that democracies did not fight one another. Essentially, when compared with the mess Washington made in the Middle East after 9/11, China policy post-2001 WTO membership took a backburner. Things weren't perfect, but they seemed fine enough.

In a great example of political scientist Edward Luttwak's "great state autism," Washington seemed to have no cognizance of how its behavior this whole time was being received in Beijing, which essentially said, "never again" and began to use its newfound wealth and industrial capacity to invest heavily in naval and missile development with the aim of establishing a new doctrine of A2AD, or area denial. This is the strategy of being able to prevent the United States from interfering in China's immediate maritime environs, specifically the south and east China sea, where it has outstanding territorial disputes with South Korea, Japan, the Philippines, Vietnam, and a few other of its neighbors. Beginning in 2012 China indeed began to escalate its claims against some of its neighbors, such as the Philippines over the Scarborough Shoals, one of which it occupied as part of its larger "island building" strategy in the Spratly's. And while this all may seem like so much obscure trivia, the United States has mutual defense treaties with several of these states. In fact, just this past week the White House warned China that it would fight them over the Philippines claims in the South China Sea if Beijing pushed things.

In the background to all this, economically, China was growing astonishingly fast during the two decades following its WTO accession, while the United States struggled in the wake of the 2001 and 2008 recessions. The financial crisis in particular had been deeply damaging. China, however, had been very helpful during the crisis, and soon thereafter became the world's second largest economy. It was at that point Washington, now under the Obama administration, put forward the idea of what was at the time called a "G-2" relationship between China and America; a strategic and economic dialogue that essentially amounted to making China America's junior partner in upholding the existing international order created by Washington since World War Two. When China declined, remaining focused on its long term goal of achieving effective independence in a multipolar world, Washington immediately thereafter set about trying to contain China. The so called "pivot to Asia" was a combination of military, diplomatic, and economic repositioning. Washington relocated assets to the Pacific; it launched a diplomatic offensive to bolster old alliances and bilateral relationships, and to build all new ones, such as the Quad, which features India, or AUKUS; the strategy also featured a new trade agreement, the Transpacific Partnership (TPP), which was meant to build around China the largest customs union in terms of GDP over the coming century and then to exclude China from it.

For all that, however, China still remained off the front pages of the papers and official talk was generally confined to public statements regarding China as a key strategic partner. In the years prior to Trump taking office, it was Iran was in Washington's crosshairs over its nuclear program, as well as Russia over its actions in Ukraine. Trump demonized China early and often, tapping into a populist vein upset over America's deindustrialization due to globalization. He began a trade war with China, the fruits of which have yet to be seen; but more importantly, the way he spoke about China, as an enemy taking advantage of America, was new to the era's political discourse. Further, his policy teams routinely churned out papers and studies singling out China as a threat that needed containing;

this was because, in the words of Trump's Secretary of State at the time Rex Tillerson: "China Threatened the U.S. Navy's Pacific Domination." As he was leaving office, Trump's second Secretary of State, Mike Pompeo, officially charged China with committing genocide against its own people, the Turkic Muslim minorities of Xinjiang. At the same time, it was leaked to the press that the United States had inserted military trainers onto Taiwan, a decision that was never publicly debated but which certainly violated the spirit if not the letter of the terms of Washington's normalization of relations with Beijing, as did a series of high level visits, including Nancy Pelosi's, which resulted in Beijing blockading the island with missile tests.

Despite his early, moderate statements regarding China, Biden ultimately followed the path trodden by Trump. In fact, in several statements he escalated it: breaking with Washington's long-held policy of "strategic ambiguity" regarding whether or not the U.S. would military intervene in the event of an attack on Taiwan, he stated in multiple public addresses that the United States would definitely intervene. Yes, today it is safe to say that Sino-American relations are decidedly hostile. In fact, the period of the Third Taiwan Strait Crisis aside, which proved a temporary blip, I would say they are at their lowest since the 1950s.

If you take a look at the slide, you'll see I write that Chinese economic growth is slowing, but that it will remain significantly faster than those of the matured and post-industrial economies of the west; further, that it is pursuing autarkic policies to insulate itself from potential attempts at western decoupling, such as sanctions, tariffs, or investment bans. Apart from its alliance with Russia, Beijing has been building alternate institutions to those created by the United States and is seeking to expand the use of its own currency in transactions with key partners. Beijing accuses Washington of trying to turn Taiwan into a powder keg, and there are perceptions on the part of the Chinese that the United States is abandoning its "One China" policy, that is the formal of the first communique "that there is but one China and that Taiwan is part of it."

Taiwan is nice, after all. It's a democracy now, and rich, and important in global supply chains. Plus, as General MacArthur observed, its essentially an unsinkable aircraft carrier 80 miles from China's cost. However, Taiwan is a red line for Beijing, whose leaders view it as the last remnant of China's century of humiliations; and it strongly opposes increased diplomatic and military exchanges between Taiwan and the United States. We've come to a dangerous place. We did so by choice. And we should all hope that the first in person talks between President Biden and President Xi, scheduled at this point for next month, are productive in trying to navigate these many dangers.

This segues nicely into my closing remarks.

I would be being insincere if I said I had no opinion on how relations with China should be handled. I do not, however, insist that you accept my interpretation of events or embrace my preferred policy prescriptions – all of which you can easily find in ten minutes of searching on the internet. What I do ask, however, as people highly statistically like to be active voters, is to think deliberately about what is being asked, what is being staked, what it is that is likely to be gained, and what other alternatives exist when it comes to Sino-American relations. Between the two of them just a fraction of their nuclear arsenals being used could wipe out human civilization in an afternoon. Even assuming a hot conflict that doesn't reach the nuclear threshold, we're talking about World War level casualties in hypothetical battles over islands less than one hundred miles from mainland China and which are officially recognized by the U.S. government as well as the United Nations as part of China.

Apart from considerations of possible war or human extinction, as an advocate of constitutional republican government, it is a fact that such a limited government is incompatible with a state powerful enough to engage in overseas adventurism and militarism as the United States does. It is economically and morally bankrupting us. In the words of Pat Buchannan, we are meant to be a republic not an empire, an example, not an enforcer.

Thank you for your time.

Chinese History up to the 19ᵗʰ Century

The purpose of the inclusion of this chapter, adapted from a pair of lectures I give at the university, is to essentially fill in some background for those readers interested in Chinese history prior to its being effectively incorporated into the general Western historical accounts, usually around the middle of the 19ᵗʰ Century and the Opium Wars. While necessarily incomplete, it being parts of a pair of lectures in a survey-level class, it nonetheless greatly expands upon the brief historical treatment included in the initial hardback version of The Fake China Threat.

The first chapter of your book focuses almost exclusively on China, its cultural history and its relations with nearby peoples, such as the Mongols, and the authors have you understand that by 1500, the beginning of the Modern Period, China was the most economically and technologically advanced polity on earth, along with being the oldest and most populous. Now this is all true. And in terms of understanding China, and particularly its incredible longevity, as you'll see here in a moment the earliest antecedents of Chinese civilization reach all the way back to the time of the Pharaohs Khufu and Khafre, the commissioners of the great Pyramids you can still see in Egypt today, China is, in the words of the now deceased American political scientist Lucien Pye, best understood historically as a civilization rather than a state. Now what I mean by that is that the territory that constituted "China" changed significantly over the millennia, as did the nature and origins of its rulers; while what remained the same, the glue if you will, its defining characteristics, were cultural: language and religion first and foremost.

Much like medieval European history then, and perhaps even more so, it is impossible to tell a neat linear story of the history of China. There is a great deal of division and interruption, with well over 50 recorded dynasties – and often there were competing dynasties coexisting simultaneously, occupying different parts of the territory of what today we call China.

So, actually, before we go any further, I'd like to direct your attention back to our PowerPoint slides, here, because what you see are a series of illustrations depicting the various territorial holdings of some of the most significant of these Chinese Imperial Dynasties, beginning with the Xia. Now, much like the founding of Rome, there is a significant degree of mythology surrounding this dynasty, in fact there is far more than in the case of Rome because it is significantly older. Indeed there is an entire school of Chinese historians who doubt its actual existence and attribute it to later dynasties seeking to justify their own rule, specifically the Zhou who we'll talk about in a moment. However, you can see several important things from this "alleged" first Dynasty. The first thing to note is its location: on the Yellow River in the north China Plain. And this is important, because even though China is to this day very much heterogeneous, with something like 50 different officially recognized ethno-linguistic groups, it is the ethnically Han, Mandarin-speaking peoples who we mean when we talk about the "Chinese." At least that's who I mean; I suppose I shouldn't speak for anyone else, but that is generally the case. And this is the area where the Han are said to have originated.

Now, this semi-mythical Xia Dynasty is alleged to have been supplanted by the Shang, who through virtuous rule and successful wars expanded the territory controlled by the burgeoning "Chinese" Empire. They are in their turn displaced by the Zhou, and one thing you note in these early historical accounts, and this is something that will recur throughout, is this idea of eventual degeneracy: that is, the initial leaders are strong, virtuous, et cetera, and then as the generations pass the leadership becomes degenerate and lose the right to rule. The Zhou were the first to allegedly formulate this idea of the "Mandate of Heaven," and it extended not just to a ruler doing a poor job ruling, but even things like natural disasters or famines occurring could be seen as an Emperor having lost the right to rule and this would provoke rebellion.

Now, these early kingdoms were patrimonial, that is not professionalized – they were essentially run by members of the

Emperor's own family, including those that had been brought in by marriage or brought in symbolically as vassals; and these would usually be powerful local, war lords, barons if you want to think about it in the medieval European context. Maintaining stability can be a challenge in that context, however, especially in an area as large as China; in the case of the Zhou, as you can see here, this was an area larger than modern day France. And a revolt among various powerful vassals leads to the Warring States Period.

Now, out of this emerges the Han Dynasty – and though it quickly breaks down, plunging the region into another period of competing kingdoms, it is significant because the territorial extent of the Empire will essentially remain unchanged as we move through the next several hundred years, essentially until the Mongols and later the Manchus roll in.

But before we talk about these foreign invasions, I'd like to talk briefly about the professionalization of the Chinese state, which occurs during the Tang and Song dynasties. Now since the reading for this week spends a considerable amount of time on this, as well as on Confucianism, which we'll talk about in just a few minutes, I'm not going to spend too much time going into the details of the imperial examinations that produced the scholar officials who staffed the Chinese Civil Service. However, I do just want to say a few things about them because they're extremely important. They began in approximately the 6th century under the Sui Dynasty, but they really take hold under the Tang dynasty which follows, and they were expanded under the Song. Generally speaking, the exams meritocratic, that is they were open to anyone regardless of their birth; and their purpose was to undermine military, aristocratic, dominance by creating a single, unifying literate administrative class whose loyalty was to the state rather than to any other group or individual. They were incredibly successful and continued, with only a few slight interruptions, until the early 20th century. While there were different levels of examination, from the local to the palatial, and had different emphases, they primarily consisted of the Confucian classics we'll be talking about on the next slide.

Now in part because of the stability that this more effective state administration brings, China becomes a center of learning, innovation, and wealth – this, combined with its relatively flat northerly geography made it a prime invasion target. However, invaders like the Mongols, who would establish the Yuan dynasty, part of the great spreading Mongol Empire we saw earlier in the lecture, these roving bandits found themselves needing to rely on the same class of Confucian, Han Chinese scholar-officials to extract all that wealth in China effectively. This is similar to what would happen later in the 19th century when the Europeans began arriving in force, but that's getting way ahead of things.

The last dynasty you see listed here is the Ming dynasty, and if you're going to write down anything about the series of dynasties that have ruled China, I would make it this: the Mongol Yuan were supplanted by the Han Ming who were supplanted by the Manchu Qing, the last Imperial Dynasty before the Republican revolution of 1912, which will mark the jumping off point for talking about the birth of Modern China. So if you are ever asked, which you will be on Thursday for your quiz: what was the last ethnically Han Chinese Imperial Dynasty you will answer, the Ming. Fun fact, the Triads, a criminal organization that exists right up to the present day had its origins as a secret society dedicated to the return of the Ming dynasty and the ouster of the ethnically foreign Manchu Qing who we'll met during our reading and in our lecture Thursday.

And this brings us to our final slide. First, you have the Great Wall – really the great Walls, as there are several stretches of wall begun and completed at different times and by different dynasties. The first section of the wall dates back to the 7th century, but most of the famous sections you would see today if you were sight-seeing were built by the Ming. Perhaps unsurprisingly given what we've just been talking about regarding its wide open northern approaches, virtually all of the sections of the wall, no matter what period they were built, were built facing northward. Next up is Kong Qui, or Confucius as we Latinized speakers call him, he's the fellow on the top right; the authors of your book spend the majority of their time actually talking about Confucius and Confucianism in their chapter on China, so I'll just add a few things here to what you'll be reading over the next day or two: the first is that despite the presence of Taoism, Buddhism, and later Islam, and despite the fact that ideologically it is probably closer to a philosophy than a religion, for our purposes it is safe to say that Confucianism was the dominant religion in China throughout the Imperial period. Indeed, even today, just recently, the Chinese Communist Party who have ruled the country since the end of the 1940s introduced a series of videos depicting Karl Marx and Confucius meeting and exchanging ideas. The other thing you might want to note, because the authors don't make this entirely clear when they cite it, is that the Analects of Confucius are a series of aphorisms later attributed to Confucius and that Confucius himself is said to have simply been preserving a set of older, classical texts by spreading their teaching. Otherwise, Allosso and Williford do a fine job as far as an introduction to the Cardinal Principles and Virtues around which Confucianism is based.

I'll return to Sinicization, the Silk Road and major Chinese innovations in just a moment; but let's first talk briefly about the fellow on the bottom left here while we're on the subject of Chinese culture: this is Sun-tzu, attributed author of the military text *the Art of War*, copies of which are still in virtually every major bookstore today. Thought to have been written somewhere in the 6th or 7th century BCE, many of the aphorisms the book contains are applicable to the present day. One of my favorites is: The greatest victory is that which requires no battle, a formulation he repeats in several different ways throughout. War is costly, both in lives and money; fighting can seriously destabilize even the most apparently secure regime, and so the wise ruler seeks to win before the fighting even commences. Think of it as warfare by prior positioning along a series of dimensions. Another classic text which is also relevant today, it was one of Mao's own personal favorites and has enjoyed a renaissance in contemporary China as Xi has attempted to lean on traditional Chinese nationalism rather than strictly Marxist ideology, the Romance of the Three Kingdoms. This is an historical novel about the fractious years of the late Han Dynasty, and it was written during the Ming Dynasty. Much like Mallory's Le Morte D'Arthur, that is the Death of Arthur, the author Luo Guanzhong was tying together a series of existing, mostly oral, stories about the period, standardizing and preserving the traditional tales.

This was occurring in the context of the transition from the Mongol Yuan Dynasty to the Han Ming Dynasty, the last and greatest of the Han Chinese Empires, and so the popularity of this retelling of ethnic Han Chinese heroism was quite understandable. On a related note, let's jump back and talk a little bit about Sinicization. Now before we do, it is worth repeating that as a survey course we're going to be speaking in generalizations, and even among academics this subject is fraught with controversy. However, generally speaking, Sinicization refers to the process of foreigners, invaders or conquered peoples, adopting culturally Han Chinese practices, things like language and religion. This was similar to the case of the Normans of medieval Europe who tended to adopt local cultures.

Finally, we have the Silk Road and Chinese innovations – let's start with the latter: the Chinese were the first to many of what would later become the most important technological advances of the Modern Period, things like gunpowder, the magnetic compass, and moveable type. The Chinese were also the largest producers of silk, and were the only producers of silk until several centuries after Christ, when a pair of monks managed to smuggle some silkworms out of China for the Byzantine Emperor Justinian. On the topic of Byzantium, the last picture on the bottom right you see is of the Silk Road, arguably the single most important artery of commerce for a millennia until the final fall of the Eastern Roman Empire, that is

Byzantium, when Constantinople was conquered by the Ottoman Turks in the 15th century – much more to say on that next week.

We'll leave off today's lecture here, with the last of the ethnically Han Chinese Imperial Dynasties comfortably ensconced in power, China the most advanced civilization, state, and economy on earth, and about to launch some famed, if brief, treasure fleets. Thursday another invasion from the north will bring on the final Imperial dynasty, the Manchu Qing, to power. They will extend Imperial China's territorial reach to its furthest ever extent, into central Asia.

***

Last time we met we talked about the origins of Chinese civilization, the Chinese polity, and the multitude of Dynasties that ruled China up to the Modern Period, that is approximately the year 1500. Today we're going to continue with China, and in fact I am going to take us slightly beyond the year 1500. The reason for this is that after today we're going to depart the Chinese narrative arc for the next several lectures, and when it intersects with the other narratives we're going to be developing in the intervening weeks, it will be more convenient for us to have moved the Chinese narrative up into the late 18th century.

So when we last left off, we were in the midst of the great Ming Dynasty, as you know from your quiz this was the last ethnically Han Chinese Imperial Dynasty. Something we weren't able to get to during the last lecture, something which makes the Ming somewhat singular from the perspective of the other Chinese Imperial Dynasties, is its period of deep water naval expeditions. Now as you can see from our slide here, Ming China has many of the characteristics of preceding Chinese Imperial Dynasties, as well as the Qing Dynasty that will follow, namely its incredibly large army, economy, and sophisticated state apparatus the early Ming featured a period of incredible shipbuilding and travel around Indian Ocean and South and East China seas. You see on the slide here a map detailing the voyages of the great Ming eunuch admiral Zheng He. Apart from noting the incredible range of some of these voyages, as you can see, they reach all the way to the eastern coast of Africa, what is today Somalia, I'd like you to just briefly note the locations of the Timurid Empire and Delhi Sultanate, as we will be talking about their successor states as we move westward later in the lecture. These voyages resulted in the expansion of the Chinese tributary system, with emissaries being brought back to the Imperial court; this political network was very loose, not like the later colonial projects of the western Europeans we'll begin looking at the week after next. That is not to say they were not highly militarized, or that these travelers to the Imperial court were always voluntary; far from it. however, the Chinese did bring things like silk, porcelain, et cetera with them, so they were in many cases welcomed – and, in any case, this foray into overseas expansion was not to last. The voyages ended in 1433 and never resumed.

Why did the Chinese stop? Why didn't they start traversing the globe setting up colonizing and converting the native populations? They had a large fleet, after all, and plenty of resources. Well, the fact is no one is entirely sure; there are several theories, however, and the combination of reasons various scholars give no doubt get near enough to the truth for our purposes: first, floating such large fleets is extremely capital intensive and it isn't as though the Chinese financial system was very sophisticated by today's standards, nor was tax collection very efficient. It just couldn't be. So there are fiscal causes. Then, the contemporary Chinese scholar Sui makes a very convincing case that the abandonment of the voyages was to a significant degree determined by bureaucratic infighting – that is the fight between different departments of the government over power and purview. Think of arguments within our own establishment in Washington DC today, between the Navy and Air Force for example – one wants a new class of destroyers the other wants more money for 5th generation fighters; or how about fights between the Department of Homeland Security and FBI over who has authority over what, cetera. The more things change the more they stay the same, as the old saw goes.

Related to the fiscal cause already detailed, it is possible the fleets were in part abandoned because of dangers on other frontiers and the need to shift resources to meet these threats. Because while the threat environment to the south was quite benign, most troubles there being internal, which we'll talk about here in a moment, you'll recall that China had been invaded many times from the north hence the location of the Great Wall. And, spoiler alert, China is going to be invaded yet again from the north very shortly here, by the Manchus, who will establish the last of the Chinese Imperial dynasties, that of the Qing, which will persist all the way through the first decade of the 20th century before finally succumbing to a variety of pressures we'll eventual talk about. So you have pressing security needs to the north. A decade after the fleet is abandoned, in fact, the Ming will fight a series of engagements with the Mongols, and then those internal problems we hinted at will crop up – the lengthy Miao Rebellions in central China also occurring during this same period, approximately the 1540s and 50s. You also had the absence of need: the treasure fleets weren't bringing back necessities. It is debated whether or not these ventures were breaking even. I tend to think not, but even if they were turning a small profit, they weren't bringing back necessities. Remember, China is arguably at its economic and technological peak of relative development; it is soon to be at its greatest territorial extent as well; but so its urge to seek new products, new markets, it just isn't at all pressing. Nor were these expeditions creating client states who could be used militarily against invaders like the Mongols or Manchus. Lastly, as mentioned by your textbook, the Chinese state religion, Confucianism, was not evangelical: there was no drive to go out proselytizing and making converts.

So, whatever the exact cause, we've listed all the main reasons generally given, the fleets are abandoned, the Ming turn inward, and as I just mentioned a little over a century later, they will be conquered by the invading Manchu – although this really isn't the correct way to think about the transition from the Ming to the Qing. Because the Qing were the descendants of the Jin Dynasty, an earlier northern Dynasty, one of the several dozen odd other Chinese Imperial dynasties that I neglected to mention during our first lecture due to the constraints of time. But I digress: what this means is that the eventual Qing Imperial leadership had been vassals off the Ming Emperor. In fact the beginning of this conflict over control of the Chinese state between the two is generally marked by the issuance by the Manchus of the Seven Grievances, which basically amounted to a declaration of war on his Lord. Think of a baron's revolt occurring and gathering steam – until, over the course of many years, decades in fact, you have to remember China even at that point is still very large, there are a lot of different clans and local power brokers that have to be dealt with apart from the Imperial forces themselves, the Qing Empire is established: in fact, although you can see here that although the Qing Empire is taken to have been established by the early 1640s it isn't until 1683 that the last Ming loyalist stronghold, Formosa, that is the island of Taiwan, about 80 miles off the coast of the mainland, is conquered and Qing rule is officially undisputed – again, the more things change the more they stay the same, as you'll see when we talk about the late 1940s and the Chinese Civil War between the forces of Chiang Kai-Shek and Mao Zedong.

Before moving on just a couple of things to note from the slide regarding the later Ming period: they grant a trading rights to the Portuguese on the island of Macau in the later 16th century. We'll talk more about that in the coming weeks when we get to the Iberian explorers. Like all empires, fiscal problems mount, unrest brews, and eventually things start to fall apart: in the language of the Chinese histories, the Ming are losing the "Mandate of Heaven," which we talked about last lecture.

But now let's transition and take a look at our slide detailing the Qing. As you can see, the Qing carried on their wars of conquest, they were a very martial people, after all, the Manchus. They were to a significant degree already Sinicized, of course, something we talked about last time and which your reading for the week mentions. But they extend the Chinese polity to its greatest territorial extent, pushing deep into central Asia in a series of campaigns during the middle of the 18th century, that is the 1700s. This is, as we will see, the apogee of Chinese Imperial power. Because as you can see on this next slide, the Manchu dynasty begins encountering a series of very serious problems around this time. Both internal and external, these problems are only going to get worse. European traders are arriving in ever greater numbers, bringing with them drugs, foreign religions – the history of Christianity in China is interesting and variegated, though hardly central prior to the 19th century; we'll talk more about that in subsequent lectures. Rebellions against the Manchu, which remember these are viewed as essential foreign occupiers are a recurring problem and one of the most serious rebellions takes place in the last decade of the 18th century, the White Lotus Rebellion – which though it is put down it comes at great cost and is one of those events which makes people wonder whether the Qing Emperor is losing the Mandate of Heaven.

But we'll leave China here at present, at the zenith of its power. It seems a nice thing to do, since when we next introduce China to the narrative, picking up right here at the beginning of the 19th century, it is going to be for quite a bit of bad news. Everything from invasion to civil war, famine, revolution invasion again, civil war again, near total destruction, famine again: the century of humiliation is, well pretty much what it sounds like. Before we do, however, I'd like to read you something I put up on this slide here; it is excerpts from a letter written on behalf of one of these Qing Emperors to the King of Great Britain at the time, in answer to British requests for trading, diplomatic, and religious rights; and I want to read it to you because I think it really gets at the heart of the kind of chauvinism I think comes naturally to great civilizations and empires, and which if you continue into historical studies you will find abounds: that is we are the greatest, most important people, ever anywhere:

You, O King, live beyond the confines of many seas, nevertheless, impelled by your humble desire to partake of the benefits of our civilisation [sic], you have dispatched a mission respectfully bearing your memorial [...] although our Celestial Empire possesses all things in prolific abundance and lacks no product within its own borders. There was therefore no need to import the manufactures of outside barbarians in exchange for our own produce. But as the tea, silk and porcelain which the Celestial Empire produces, are absolute necessities to European nations and to yourselves, we have permitted, as a signal mark of favour [sic], that foreign *hongs* [merchant firms] should be established at Canton, so that your wants might be supplied and your country thus participate in our beneficence [....] The distinction between Chinese and barbarian is most strict, and your Ambassador's request that barbarians shall be given full liberty to disseminate their religion is utterly unreasonable.

The Fake China Threat and the Future of American Freedom: or War as the Health of the State

This talk was delivered at an event for the release of the paperback edition of The Fake China Threat and Its Very Real Danger *at Stirling Books in Albion, MI.*

I want to begin this brief address on the relationship between restrictions on individual liberty by the state on the one hand and war or intense security competition between states on the other, with a few passages from someone you'll all be familiar with, or likely be familiar with; indeed, he is often heralded, appropriately so in my opinion, as a father of the modern "conservative" movement in the United States and as an intellectual leader of the Republican Party in the latter half of the 20th century. The following excerpts come from a 1952 article for *Commonweal Magazine* entitled "A Young Republican: the Party and the Deep Blue Sea," in which William F. Buckley, founder of the *National Review*, expressed the following sentiments:

> Deeming Soviet power to be a menace to American Freedom [...] we shall have to rearrange, sensibly, our battle plans; and this means that we have got to accept Big Government for the duration [of the Cold War contest] [...] for neither an offensive nor a defensive war can be waged [...] except through the instrument of a totalitarian bureaucracy within our shores [...and that conservatives and Republicans specifically must] support large armies and air forces, atomic energy, central intelligence, war production boards and the attendant centralization of power in Washington.

For, he argued, it was better to lose our freedoms to an "ignoramus from Missouri" than a "bandit from Georgia," those references being to then President Harry Truman and Soviet leader Josef Stalin respectively; that is, it is better to surrender the classically liberal American heritage of limited government to domestic rather than foreign tyrants, and to embrace instead freedom, individualism, and constitutionalism, central banking, a domestic spying apparatus, bloated bureaucracy, welfare programs, and permanent arms industry.

To be sure, Buckley made sure to properly bemoan this alleged necessity, citing in his article all the appropriate luminaries of what the Austrian School economist Murray Rothbard would later call the "Old Right," from Albert Nock to H.L. Mencken. "Ideally," Buckley wrote, "the Republican Party Platform should acknowledge a domestic enemy, [that is] the state." But, in his words, such "idealism" must be set aside in the name of national security.

The formula, to you educated people in the here and now tragically familiar, at least I hope: "They hate us for our freedom – it is that which we must sacrifice in order to safeguard…our freedom."

Far from being just another laughable Bushism, this sad remark is the history of the United States since the dawn of the 20th century, the century of almost permanent war, hot or cold: In the words of the great libertarian intellectual Robert Higgs, "War is the master key of the state" – emergency its mandate. In fact, Dr. Higgs has written several very excellent histories in which he charts the growth of government power in the United States, showing how it almost as a rule always coincided with periods of war, declared or otherwise.

In the words of Randolph Bourne, a left-wing antiwar activist in the early 20th century: "War is the health of the state."

This relationship, between war, the preparation for war, and the loss of individual freedom to government, is so obvious one can find any number of such quotations to this effect – even if this common sense wisdom does, in the day to day bustle of life and the thousand decisions that entails, too often get lost, shuffled into the background, provisions violating our most fundamental rights stuffed into the footnotes bills thousands of pages long and passed without ever having been read – such as the 2012 National Defense Authorization Act, which contained a to this point unused but still active provision allowing for the arrest and indeterminate detention of "U.S. persons" by the U.S. military. Other times, as in the case of the Patriot Act, many of the most egregious aspects of which are still alive and well today, these were passed to tumultuous applause by masses either so deluded as to believe sacrificing their freedom makes them free or else too scared to even think at all – I could spend an hour talking just about the abuses of the NSA following the passage of the 2007 "Protect America Act," the PRISM program, or the FISC.

Large scale cooperative interaction requires trust; lies of the kind Washington has employed in pursuit of its foreign policy objectives, from reordering the Middle East to better secure Israel's interests, which didn't work, to provoking a fight with Russia over Ukraine, which also didn't work, to pervasively spying on and lying to Americans, obviously, destroy that trust; but as these policies, so near and dear to the state, can only be maintained by lies truth becomes a kind of treason: hence, in our new age of democratized media, where a call to someone upstairs at the *New York Times* from the White House can still keep a story off the front pages, or effectively spun into a kind of confused irrelevance, we see the rise of so-called "mal-information," that is true but inconvenient facts that need suppressing. Using the screen of big tech to do the dirty work, its cozy relationship with the government so open Georgetown professors sitting on the Council of Foreign Relations can now unabashedly chronicle it, we are increasingly headed for a digital panopticon that makes the efforts of the east German Stasi look absolutely laughable by comparison.

The newest justification for these policies is, of course, the Fake China Threat: the preposterous notion that China is on the cusp of taking over America or the world, that they've stolen all the jobs and technology (which Washington's policies actually sent over there, and which corporate), created an opioid crisis in rural America (again one of Washington's own failed policies blowing up its, and our, faces), and, most ridiculously of all, are making Washington look bad by publicly disagreeing with Washington's Middle East policies and undermining its policies aims elsewhere, by disagreeing over Ukraine, for example.

In opening, I chose to pick on the Republicans because it is they who, in the 20th century and on into the 21st, have seemingly always been the first and loudest to cry about "the growth of big government," "infringements on our liberties," et cetera; however, as I will show, the project, especially since the Second World War, has been a thoroughly bipartisan one.

In some ways, this goes all the way back to the founding decades of the Republic – in 1798 the Alien and Sedition Acts were passed, which effectively criminalized criticism of the government by suppressing pro-French sentiments during a conflict between the United States and France, the so-called Quasi War. The Civil War, of course, brought even more egregious violations of liberal values: in 1861 Lincoln suspended the writ of habeas corpus, that is he granted the military the authority to arrest and detain individuals indefinitely without trial; and then, even more terrible, in 1863, the radical Republican Congress passes and Lincoln signs the so-called "Enrollment Act" – got to love the government and those euphemisms, who could object to "enrollment" after all? What is that anyway? It was the establishment of forced labor, of conscription, of forcing men under penalty of the loss of their freedom to go and kill in the name of, um, freedom.

The defense of these, and the actions to come, are always the same: they are necessary to safeguard your freedom, not Washington's power.

Woodrow Wilson, one of the worst presidents we've ever had, went farther – apart from establishing the Federal Reserve, which has eroded the purchasing power of the dollar to virtually nothing, and making permanent the income tax, he denied there were even such things as "unwilling" draftees. The draftees being Americans, and Americans being represented by Congress, and Congress having passed his new, desired conscription act, no one could be said to be being taken unwillingly into the government's service. Wilson went still further, creating a Committee on Public Information (CPI), also known as the Creel Commission, in order to generate the necessary public support to take the country into World War One – a totally pointless conflict that wrecked Europe and had nothing to do with America at all. George Creel, the man Wilson personally chose to head this overt propaganda office, that word hadn't yet acquired its negative connotations, Creel and his team utilized various forms of media, including newspapers, posters, films, and pamphlets, to promote patriotic sentiment, but they also engaged in extensive censorship, stifling dissent and criticism of the government's war policies. It promoted a fervent atmosphere of patriotism and conformity, leading to the suppression of anti-war sentiments and the curtailment of free speech. The Espionage Act of 1917 and the Sedition Act of 1918 further contributed to the erosion of civil liberties, as individuals faced prosecution for expressing opinions perceived as disloyal or undermining the war effort.

Once again, it was made a crime to disagree with the government. And while the Sedition Act was allowed to lapse once the war had ended, the Espionage Act would survive and indeed many of its provisions remain to his day – though as we know from many brave leakers over the past twenty years, agencies like the NSA have gone far beyond anything anyone could have imagined in the 1910s.

World War II featured similar efforts at manipulating public opinion. The Office of War Information (OWI) was established in 1942 to coordinate wartime propaganda efforts. The OWI produced a variety of materials, including posters, films, and radio broadcasts, to maintain public support for the war, encourage enlistment, and promote war bond sales. While the U.S. propaganda efforts were generally less coercive than during World War I, they still aimed at fostering a strong sense of national unity and patriotism. Of course, the propaganda effort in this case didn't need to be quite so strong as the Japanese had clearly and viciously attacked the United States, and then Hitler had, pretty inexplicably to this very day, decided to declare war on the United States, giving Roosevelt the entry into the European War he had actually wanted. However, in terms of taking a wider view of the manipulation of events, and of public opinion, I'll let Harry Stimson, FDR's Secretary of War, have the last word, writing in his diary, which was later submitted as part of a Congressional Testimony, the insanely tedious records of which you can read for yourself, all ten thousand pages, read, in part, "Spent the evening talking the President, the great difficulty being how to maneuver the Japanese into being seen as having fired the first shot without allowing too much danger to ourselves."

But wait a second, you might be saying, these were all Democrat policies – okay, there was Teddy Roosevelt and Henry Cabot Lodge, powerful early 20th century Republicans who were avidly imperialist, but how did we get from the so-called isolationist Republicans of World War II to George W. Bush? That is quite a jump, and Richard Nixon is a good halfway point – something in itself instructive, because Nixon was a creature of the forces that took over the Republican party in the late 1940s and early 1950s. This, of course, gets us back to where I began this little talk, belittling Bill Buckley for his part in destroying what opposition there was to putting the United States on a permanent war footing, creating a permanent arms industry, sprawling alliance network of dependencies, and endless government programs and bureaucracies – and all justified based on the exaggerated threat supposedly posed to America by the Soviet Union.

The concentrated benefits and diffuse costs of these programs meant that even after it was so evident that the Soviet's couldn't possibly pose any threat to the United States that it was frankly admitted, the policies continued: Through disastrous wars in Asia of unimaginable brutality, in Korea and Vietnam, support of the bloodiest dictatorships you can imagine, like in Indonesia, and the fostering of Islamic fundamentalism as a counterweight to secular Arab nationalism – and later as a weapon against the Soviet Union in central Asia; through domestic government spying initiatives, such as COINTELPRO, a series of covert and often illegal projects conducted by the FBI from 1956 to 1971, whose main objective was to surveil, infiltrate, discredit, and disrupt domestic political organizations deemed as subversive or radical; through the end of the MAD logic of the end of the Cold War in the late 1980s – these policies continued. And once their alleged raison d'etre, the existence of the Soviet Union, vanished in the early 1990s, reasons were found to continue the same policies: Its hundreds of billions of dollars a year we're talking about, after all, and the kind of power and purview the framers of the U.S. Constitution were right to fear and distrust: power corrupts, and in the words of the late Libertarian history Ralph Raico, the 20th century was the century of the state, the century of the Nietzschean will to power, to dominate and impose and control others.

Russell Kirk, author of the Conservative Mind and a true luminary of classical liberalism, in a series of Heritage Foundation lectures on the "errors" being made at the end of the 20th century, had these critical and insightful words to say as George Bush Sr. was plowing ahead with the First Iraq War – a conflict essentially in support of British interests in Kuwaiti debt and oil leases as well as Saudi security concerns, but also probably the result of a miscommunication between Washington and one of its Middle East proxies against the Iranians, Sadam Hussein – a war which ultimately resulted in the permanent stationing of troops in Saudi Arabia, which along with support for Israeli policies toward the Palestinians formed the core of Bin Laden's grievance against the United States, ultimately culminating in 9/11, thus kicking off the war on terror, 6 trillion dollars of wasted money, the patriot act, black site torture facilities, et cetera...

But anyway, back to Russel Kirk and his wisdom: moved by "sorrow rather than wrath," he lamented that despite the death of the former imperial powers of Europe, there "remains an American Empire, still growing" through the "acquisition of client states," whose "heavy belligerent domination" would foster a "widespread impulse to pull down the imperial power," and that eventually, like the Soviets, Napoleon, or King George, "the task of repression" would be "to much to bear." And that the "Perpetual War for Peace" would produce conditions not dissimilar to those of George Orwell's 1984 – dissent criminalized, the American people impoverished, the state almighty.

And this gets to the heart of the matter: for what is at stake vis a vis China is not America's freedom, its existence, the lives, livelihoods, or prosperity of its people; what is at stake, the real thing China threatens is, in the words of then Secretary of State Rex Tillerson, quoted by Bob Woodward, is the U.S. Navy's complete "domination of the Pacific" right up to the shores of China itself.

Beyond the empty rhetoric of democracy promotion, the U.S. has and still does partner with the most vicious of tyrants so long as they acquiesce to Washington's security prerogatives, just look at Egypt, this is what you are being asked to fight and die for, to send your sons and daughters to fight over, to risk the destruction of all life on earth over: so a bunch of admirals can get new ships, so think tank flunkies funded by foreign governments don't have to get real jobs, and defense contractors and their shareholders continue to be well paid.

In the words of Scott Horton, it is understandable but unacceptable.

And if it continues, the fault will be our own – for continuing to elect Democrats and Republicans who, whatever else they disagree on, agree that nodding along and taking money from defense contractors and foreign government lobbyists is a lot easier than doing the actual work of policy making on behalf of the American people.

To return to where I began this lecture, by picking on William Buckley, he opts in the above essay to bring the American founder Thomas Jefferson into the discussion, quoting him. He would have done better to remember his Franklin: "Those who would trade their freedom for security will wind up with neither."

But then, that would have defeated the entire purpose of his apology for the state, its expanding power, and U.S. militarism abroad – which has bankrupted us morally as well as economically, making us less safe, less free, and has brought us to the edge of destruction.

We would do well, ironically, to recall the words of Abraham Lincoln, to be confident in ourselves, the strength of our positions and the rightness of the path laid out for us long ago, to follow in the name of realizing liberty in one land, these United States:

> Shall we expect some transatlantic military giant to step the ocean and crush us at a blow? Never! All the armies of Europe, Asia, and Africa combined, with all the treasure of the earth (our own excepted) in their military chest, with a Bonaparte for a commander, could not by force take a drink from the Ohio or make a track on the Blue Ridge in a trial of a thousand years. At what point then is the approach of danger to be expected? I answer. If it ever reach us it must spring up amongst us; it cannot come from abroad. If destruction be our lot we must ourselves be its author and finisher. As a nation of free men we will live forever or die by suicide.

Thank you.

Quotes

In consulting with Keith Knight, the Managing Editor of the Libertarian Institute, we determined that it would be well to include a section of various quotations at the end of *The Fake China Threat*. These span the gamut, from the warnings of early American presidents to later justifications, even paeans, to burgeoning empire.

Against the insidious wiles of foreign influence (I conjure you to believe me, fellow citizens) the jealousy of a free people ought to be constantly awake, since history and experience prove that foreign influence is one of the most baneful foes of republican government. But that jealousy to be useful must be impartial; else it becomes the instrument of the very influence to be avoided, instead of a defense against it. Excessive partiality for one foreign nation and excessive dislike of another cause those whom they actuate to see danger only on one side, and serve to veil and even second the arts of influence on the other. Real patriots who may resist the intrigues of the favorite are liable to become suspected and odious, while its tools and dupes usurp the applause and confidence of the people, to surrender their interests. The great rule of conduct for us in regard to foreign nations is in extending our commercial relations, to have with them as little political connection as possible. So far as we have already formed engagements, let them be fulfilled with perfect good faith. Here let us stop.

– George Washington, in his Farwell Address, 1796.

She has, in the lapse of nearly half a century, without a single exception, respected the independence of other nations while asserting and maintaining her own. She has abstained from interference in the concerns of others, even when conflict has been for principles to which she clings, as to the last vital drop that visits the heart. She has seen that probably for centuries to come, all the contests of that Aceldama the European world, will be contests of inveterate power, and emerging right. Wherever the standard of freedom and Independence has been or shall be unfurled, there will her heart, her benedictions and her prayers be. But she goes not abroad, in search of monsters to destroy. She is the well-wisher to the freedom and independence of all. She is the champion and vindicator only of her own.

> – John Quincy Adams, then Secretary of State,
> in a speech to the U.S. House of Representatives, 1821.

We should consider any attempt on their part to extend their system to any portion of this hemisphere as dangerous to our peace and safety.

> – James Monroe, in his Seventh Annual Address to Congress, 1823.

[It is] our manifest destiny to overspread the continent allotted by Providence for the free development of our yearly multiplying millions.

> – John L. O'Sullivan, in his article "Annexation,"
> published in the *Democratic Review*, 1845.

The war was an act of criminal aggression. I conscientiously believe that the order of annexation itself, whether it be with, or without Mexico, was unconstitutional, revolutionary, and therefore void.

> – Abraham Lincoln, then Congressman from Illinois,
> in the U.S. House of Representatives, 1848.

We regard it [Cuba] as a desirable acquisition; and we should be recreant to our duty, be unworthy of our gallant forefathers, and commit base treason against our posterity, did we relinquish our claim to it.

> – Senator Albert G. Brown of Mississippi, in the U.S. Senate, 1858.

I don't go so far as to think that the only good Indians are dead Indians, but I believe nine out of every ten are.

> – General Philip Sheridan, 1869.

The opposition [the American Anti-Imperialist League] tells us that we ought not to govern a people without their consent. I answer, the rule of liberty that all just government derives its authority from the consent of the governed, applies only to those who are capable of self-government. We govern the Indians without their consent; we govern our Territories without their consent; we govern our children without their consent... We cannot retreat from any soil where Providence has unfurled our banner.

> – Albert J. Beveridge, future Senator from Indiana,
> "The March of the Flag," 1898.

The Spanish-American War was but an incident of a general movement of expansion which had its roots in the changed environment of an industrial capacity far beyond our domestic powers of consumption. It was seen to be necessary for us not only to find foreign purchasers for our goods, but to provide the means of making access to foreign markets easy, economical and safe.

> – Emory R. Johnson, Chief of the Bureau of Foreign Commerce,
> at the U.S. Commerce Department, 1902.

Since trade ignores national boundaries and the manufacturer insists on having the world as a market, the flag of his nation must follow him, and the doors of the nations which are closed against him must be battered down. Concessions obtained by financiers must be safeguarded by ministers of state, even if the sovereignty of unwilling nations be outraged int reprocess.

> – Woodrow Wilson, 1919,
> in Noam Chomsky's *Power and Ideology*, 2015.

Gentlemen, you have no idea what it is like to be an empire on which the sun has set. The United States is the last empire, the greatest and the least shackled by tradition. It has got to accept the burdens of empire, as we have done in the past, and pick up the torch of empire from our still cooling fingers.

> – Sir Ronald Henry Amherst Storrs, British Ambassador to Greece, 1947.

Mr. President, the only way you are ever going to get this [aid to help Turkey and Greece in their fight against local communist groups] is to make a speech and scare the hell out of the country.

> – Senator Arthur Vandenberg of Michigan to President Harry Truman, 1947.

We have about 50 percent of the world's wealth but only 6.3 percent of its population... In this situation, we cannot fail to be the object of envy and resentment. Our real task in the coming period is to devise a pattern of relationships which will permit us to maintain this position of disparity without positive detriment to our own national security.

> – George Kennan, Policy Planning Study 23, 1948.

[The government] were forced to portray the Reds as "island hopping" their way to the United States... [For] if the Reds take Formosa, they will be one island nearer to the United States. It is an age-old story: a peaceful Pacific "moat" is needed for our defense. In order to protect this moat, we must secure friendly countries or bases all around it. To protect Japan and the Philippines, we must defend Formosa, to protect Formosa we must defend the Pescadores. To protect the Pescadores, we must defend Quemoy, an island three miles off the Chinese mainland. To protect Quemoy we must equip Chiang's troops for an invasion of the mainland. Where does this process end? Logically, never.

> – Murray Rothbard, writing pseudonymously
> in *Faith and Freedom*, 1955.

[Historically] American makers of plowshares could, with time and as required, make swords as well. But now we can no longer risk emergency improvisation of national defense; we have been compelled to create a permanent armaments industry of vast proportions... This conjuncture of an immense military establishment and a large arms industry is new in the American experience... Yet we must not fail to comprehend its grave implications... In the councils of government, we must guard against the acquisition of unwarranted influence, whether sought or unsought, by the military-industrial complex. The potential for the disastrous rise of misplaced power exists and will persist.

> – Dwight D. Eisenhower, in his Farewell Address, 1961.

I am concerned for the security of our great nation, not so much because of any threat from without, but because of the insidious forces working from within.

> – General Douglas MacArthur, in his Address
> to the United States Military Academy, 1962.

Were the Soviet Union to sink tomorrow under the waters of the ocean, the American military-industrial complex would have to remain, substantially unchanged, until some other adversary could be invented. Anything else would be an unacceptable shock to the American economy.

> – George Kennan, *At Century's Ending: Reflections, 1982–1995*, 1997.

War made the state, and the state makes war.

> – Charles Tilly, *Coercion, Capital, and European States*, 1990.

We have before us the opportunity to forge for ourselves and for future generations a New World Order — a world where the rule of law, not the law of the jungle, governs the conduct of nations.

> – George H.W. Bush, in his Address to Congress
> on the Persian Gulf Crisis, 1990.

A stable and prosperous China is an essential part of our vision of a more secure and prosperous world for us all.

> – Bill Clinton, in his remarks at the welcoming ceremony
> for President of China Jiang Zemin, 1997.

China is not a threat, but rather an opportunity.

> – Secretary of State Condoleezza Rice,
> in her remarks at the U.S. Naval Academy, 2005.

The United States welcomes the rise of a prosperous, peaceful, and stable China.

> – Barack Obama, in his remarks at the APEC CEO Summit, 2011.

We reject any suggestion that the United States is trying to contain or counter China.

> – National Security Advisor Susan Rice,
> in her remarks at Georgetown University, 2013.

We want China to succeed. We welcome a thriving, responsible, and peaceful China.

> – Secretary of State John Kerry,
> in his remarks at the East-West Center, 2014.

We can't continue to allow China to rape our country, and that's what they're doing.

> – Donald Trump, in a campaign rally speech, 2016.

We are ready to work with the United States to enhance communication, deepen cooperation, and properly manage differences. We should respect each other's core interests and major concerns, strengthen strategic mutual trust, and avoid strategic misjudgment.

> – Xi Jinping, in a speech at the opening of the
> 19th National Congress of the Communist Party of China, 2017.

We are willing to create a vast space for peaceful reunification, but we will never leave any room for any sort of Taiwan independence separatist activities.

> – Xi Jinping, in a speech at the opening of the
> 19th National Congress of the Communist Party of China, 2017.

We are an independent country already, and we call ourselves the Republic of China (Taiwan).

> – President Tsai Ing-wen of the Republic of China,
> in an interview with the BBC, 2019.

China is going to eat our lunch? Come on, man... They're not competition for us.

> – Joe Biden, in a campaign rally speech, 2019.

China is challenging America's predominance, and it's doing so not only economically but militarily... We need to push back on Beijing and work to get more of our allies to starting to perceive China as a global threat much like we do.

> – Secretary of Defense Mark Esper,
> in an interview with the *Washington Post*, 2019.

The China Threat is real; it's persistent; it's not going away... The intelligence is clear: Beijing intends to dominate the U.S. and the rest of the planet economically, militarily, and technologically.

> – Director of National Intelligence John Ratcliffe,
> in a *Wall Street Journal* op-ed, 2020.

We've seen China's true intentions. They want to be the dominant global military and economic power.

> – Secretary of State Mike Pompeo,
> in his remarks at the Nixon Library, 2020.

China is engaged in a whole-of-state effort to become the world's only superpower by any means necessary.

> – FBI Director Christopher Wray, at the Hudson Institute, 2020.

We're in a competition with China and other countries to win the 21st century.

> – Joe Biden, at the U.S. State Department, 2021.

Yes.

> – Joe Biden, multiple times since taking office, when asked whether the U.S. would intervene in the event of an attack on Taiwan by mainland China.

If you know nothing, you'll fall for anything.

> – Director of the Libertarian Institute Scott Horton, in a speech on the Russia-Ukraine War, 2022.

Works Cited

Amelia Browne, "Desertification in China: Causes, Impacts, and Solutions," Earth.org., December 20, 2022. earth.org/desertification-in-china.

Asia Matters for America, "How Does China's Appetite for Meat Affect the United States? — Asia Matters for America," November 22, 2021. asiamattersforamerica.org/articles/how-does-chinas-appetite-for-meat-affect-the-united-states.

Associated Press, "China Cuts Uighur Births with IUDs, Abortion, and Sterilization," *Denver Post*, June 29, 2020. denverpost.com/2020/06/29/china-cuts-uighur-births.

Campbell, Charlie, "China's Aging Population Is a Major Threat to Its Future," *Time*, February 7, 2019. time.com/5523805/china-aging-population-working-age.

Cancian, Mark F., Matthew Cancian, and Eric Heginbotham. "The First Battle of the Next War: Wargaming a Chinese Invasion of Taiwan," January 27, 2023. csis.org/analysis/first-battle-next-war-wargaming-chinese-invasion-taiwan.

Chase, Michael et al., "China's Incomplete Military Transformation," Rand Corporation, 2015. rand.org/content/dam/rand/pubs/research_reports/RR800/RR893/RAND_RR893.pdf.

"China Natural Gas Reserves, Production and Consumption Statistics," Worldometers, n.d. worldometers.info/gas/china-natural-gas.

"China Oil Reserves, Production and Consumption Statistics," Worldometers, n.d. worldometers.info/oil/china-oil.

"China's $6 Trillion Hidden Debt Gets Stress-Tested in Downturn," Bloomberg News, November 17, 2021. bloomberg.com/news/articles/2021-11-17/china-s-6-trillion-hidden-debt-gets-stress-tested-in-downturn.

Clemons, Steve, "The U.S. would destroy Taiwan's chip plants if China invades, says former Trump official," Semafor, March 13, 2023. semafor.com/article/03/13/2023/the-us-would-destroy-taiwans-chip-plants-if-china-invades-says-former-trump-official.

Colliers, Andrew, *China's Technology War: Why Beijing Took Down its Tech Giants* (London: Palgrave MacMillan, 2022).

Dress, Brad (2023). "Here's where U.S. military will open bases in the Philippines in move to counter China," *The Hill*, April 3.

Farrell and Newman (2023). *Underground Empire: How America Weaponized the World Economy*, Henry Holt and Co: New York.

Fay, Peter, *The Opium War (1840–1842): Barbarians in the Celestial Empire in the Early Part of the Nineteenth Century and the War by Which They Forced Her Gates Ajar* (Chapel Hill: University of North Carolina Press, 1998).

Freeman, Ben (2022). "How the Taiwan Lobby Helped Pave the Way for Pelosi's Trip," *Responsible Statecraft*, the Quincy Institute.

French, Paul, *Betrayal in Paris: How the Treaty of Versailles Led to China's Long Revolution* (London: Penguin, 2016).

Gaddis, John, *The United States and the Origins of the Cold War (1941–47)* (New York: Columbia University Press, 2000).

Goldstein, Lyle (2017). "The US-China Naval Balance in the Asia-Pacific: An Overview," *The China Quarterly*, Cambridge University Press, Vol. 232.

Gomez and Mistreanu (2023). "US renews warning it will defend Philippines after incidents with Chinese Vessels in South China Sea," Associated Press, October 23.

Haijian, Mao, *The Qing Empire and the Opium War: The Collapse of the Heavenly Dynasty* (Cambridge: Cambridge University Press, 2018).

Hesketh et al., "The Consequences of Son Preference and Sex-Selective Abortion in China and other Asian Countries," *Canadian Medical Association Journal*. Published September 6, 2011; Volume 183 (12): pp. 1374–77.

Holland, Bose, and Hunnicutt (2024). "U.S. does not support Taiwan independence, Biden says," *Reuters*, January 13.

Hoopes, Townsend and Douglas Brinkley, *FDR and the Creation of the U.N.* (New Haven: Yale University Press, 1997).

Hsiao, Russell (2021). "Taiwanese Preference for Status Quo Remains Constant Even as Views Harden," Global Taiwan Brief, Vol. 6, Issue 15.

Hung, Ho-fung, *The China Boom: Why China Will Not Rule the World* (New York: Columbia University Press, 2017).

Huntington, Samuel, *The Clash of Civilizations and the Remaking of World Order* (New York: Simon Schuster, 1996).

Ignatius, David, "The Inside Story of how the U.S. Shot Down the Chinese Balloon," *Washington Post*, February 4, 2023. washingtonpost.com/opinions/2023/02/04/chinese-balloon-pentagon-intelligence-details.

Ji, You, "Dealing with the Malacca Dilemma: China's Effort to Protect its Energy Supply," *Strategic Analysis*, September 18, 2007. tandfonline.com/doi/abs/10.1080/09700160701415743.

Kissinger, Henry, *On China* (London: Penguin, 2011).

Lee, Amanda, "China Debt: Has It Changed in 2021 and How Big Is It Now?" *South China Post*, June 5, 2021. scmp.com/economy/china-economy/article/3135883/china-debt-has-it-changed-2021-and-how-big-it-now.

Lee, James, "The One-China Policy in Transition," *Georgetown Journal of International Affairs*, November 7, 2022. https://gjia.georgetown.edu/2022/11/07/the-one-china-policy-in-transition.

Li, Danhui and Xafeng Xia, *Mao and the Sino-Soviet Split, 1959–1973: A New History* (Cambridge: Harvard University Press, 2020).

Liang, Qiao and Wang Xiangsui, *Unrestricted Warfare* (Panama City: Pan American Publishing Company, 1999).

Lien-sheng, Yang, "Historical Notes on the Chinese World Order," *The Chinese World Order: Traditional China's Foreign Relations* (Cambridge: Harvard University Press, 1968).

Lynch, Michael, *The Chinese Civil War (1945–49)* (Oxford: Osprey Press, 2010).

Magnus, George, *Red Flags: Why Xi's China is in Jeopardy* (New Haven: Yale University Press, 2018).

McCaul, Michael. "Best Deterrence to Xi in Taiwan is Failure for Putin in Ukraine." Chuck Todd, *Meet the Press*, April 8, 2023.

McKinney and Harris (2021). "Broken Nest: Deterring China from Invading Taiwan," *US Army War College Quarterly: Parameters*, Vol. 51 No. 4.

McMahon, Dinny, *China's Great Wall of Debt: Shadow Banks, Ghost Cities, Massive Loans, and the End of the Chinese Miracle* (New York: Harper's Business Press, 2018).

Nakashima et al., "Chinese Balloon Part of Vast Aerial Surveillance Program, U.S. Says," *Washington Post*, February 7, 2023.

"Office of the Historian," n.d. history.state.gov.

Panda, Ankit (2019). "In Philippines, Pompeo Offers Major Alliance Assurance on South China Sea," *The Diplomat*.

Porter, Gareth and Max Blumenthal, "U.S. State Department Accusation of China 'Genocide' Relied on Data Abuse and Baseless Claims by Far-Right Ideologue," *Grayzone*, February 18, 2021. thegrayzone.com/2021/02/18/us-media-reports-chinese-genocide-relied-on-fraudulent-far-right-researcher.

Putz, Catherine. "Which Countries Are For or Against China's Xinjiang Policies?" *The Diplomat*, July 15, 2019. thediplomat.com/2020/10/2020-edition-which-countries-are-for-or-against-chinas-xinjiang-policies.

Raimondo, Justin, "Looking at the 'Big Picture,' Libertarian Realism: A Theory of Foreign Relations," Antiwar.com, November 10, 2011. original.antiwar.com/justin/2011/11/10/looking-at-the%c2%a0big-picture.

Rudd, Kevin, *The Avoidable War? The Dangers of a Catastrophic Conflict between the U.S. and China* (New York: Public Affairs, 2022).

Sevastopulo and Hille (2023). "Washinton presses Taiwan presidential frontrunner on White House Comments," *Financial Times*, July 19.

Shambough, David, "China's Military in Transition: Politics, Professionalism, Procurement, and Power Projection," *The China Quarterly*, June 1996.

Shepherd, Christian, "China's Foreign Minister Predicts Impending Clash with the United States," *Washington Post*, March 7, 2023. washingtonpost.com/world/2023/03/07/china-us-foreign-minister-taiwan-russia.

Shih, Victor C., *Economic Shocks and Authoritarian Stability* (Ann Arbor: University of Michigan Press, 2020).

Statista. "Per Capita Living Space in China in Urban and Rural Areas 2002–2019," September 15, 2022. statista.com/statistics/225016/per-capita-living-space-in-china-in-urban-and-rural-areas.

Trading Economics. "China Money Supply M2 – May 2023 Data – 1996–2022 Historical – June Forecast," n.d. tradingeconomics.com/china/money-supply-m2.

Trading Economics. "United States Money Supply M2 – May 2023 Data – 1959–2022 Historical – June Forecast," n.d. tradingeconomics.com/united-states/money-supply-m2.

U.S. Congress, *Hearings Before the Joint Committee on the Investigation of the Pearl Harbor Attack* (Washington, 1946): p. 5433.

Van de Ven, Hans, *China at War: Triumph and Tragedy in the Emergence of the New China* (Cambridge: Harvard University Press, 2018).

Waley, Arthur, *The Opium War through Chinese Eyes* (Stanford: Stanford University Press, 1958).

Westad, Odd Arne, *Decisive Encounters: The Chinese Civil War (1946–50)* (Stanford: Stanford University Press, 2003).

Wildau, Gabriel, "Prominent China Debt Bear Warns of $6.8 Trillion in Hidden Losses," *Financial Times*, August 16, 2017. ft.com/content/3bc4da08-8171-11e7-a4ce-15b2513cb3ff.

Willick, Jason (2024). "Why a Taiwan election upset could be a U.S. blessing," *Washington Post*, January 5.

World Bank Open Data. "World Bank Open Data," n.d. data.worldbank.org/indicator/AG.LND.ARBL.HA.PC.

Yevodyeva, M.G., "Development of the Chinese A2/AD System in the Context of U.S.-China Relations," *Herald of the Russian Academy of Sciences*, September 29, 2022.

Zagoria, Donald, *The Sino-Soviet Conflict (1956–61): The Widening Breach Between the Russian and Chinese Communists* (Cambridge: Athenaeum Press, 1964).

Zhang and Freeman (2021). "The Taiwan Lobby," Center for International Policy, Foreign Influence and Transparency Initiative.

Lastly, here is a link to a PDF of the Three Communiques: choices.edu/wp-content/uploads/2017/08/choices-china-US-china.pdf.

The Libertarian Institute

Check out the Libertarian Institute at LibertarianInstitute.org. It's Scott Horton, Sheldon Richman, Laurie Calhoun, James Bovard, Kyle Anzalone, Connor Freeman, Keith Knight and the best libertarian writers and podcast hosts on the Internet. We are a 501(c)(3) tax-exempt charitable organization. EIN 83-2869616.

Help support our efforts — including our project to purchase wholesale copies of this book to send to important congressmen and women, antiwar groups and influential people in the media. We don't have a big marketing department to push this effort. We need your help to do it. And thank you.

LibertarianInstitute.org/donate or
The Libertarian Institute
612 W. 34th St.
Austin, TX 78705

Check out all of our other great Libertarian Institute books at LibertarianInstitute.org/books:

Hotter Than the Sun: Time to Abolish Nuclear Weapons by Scott Horton
Enough Already: Time to End the War on Terrorism by Scott Horton
Questioning the COVID Company Line: Critical Thinking in Hysterical Times by Laurie Calhoun
Fool's Errand: Time to End the War in Afghanistan by Scott Horton
Voluntaryist Handbook by Keith Knight
Israel: Winner of the 2003 Iraq Oil War by Gary Vogler
The Great Ron Paul: The Scott Horton Show Interviews 2004–2019
No Quarter: The Ravings of William Norman Grigg, edited by Tom Eddlem
Coming to Palestine by Sheldon Richman
What Social Animals Owe to Each Other by Sheldon Richman

Keep a look out for more great titles to be published in 2023 and 2024.

Made in the USA
Middletown, DE
02 February 2024

49007816R00086